TOSCANINI

TOSCANINI

THE MAESTRO: A LIFE IN PICTURES

Edited by | Foreword by
MARCO CAPRA | **ANTONIO PAPPANO**

Rizzoli
NEW YORK

New York · Paris · London · Milan

CONTENTS

ARTURO TOSCANINI, ITALIAN TITAN 17

Antonio Pappano

MUSIC AS A MISSION

A Sorcerer, a Miracle Worker. Toscanini and the Search for Authenticity 23

Music's new lease on life. Toscanini and Puccini 41

Wagner's influence. Toscanini and the "Greatest Composer of the Century" 57

Busseto Akin to Bayreuth. Toscanini for Verdi 75

GLOBAL CHARISMA

Passion and intransigence. The Legend of Toscanini 91

Against the Tyranny of Fascism. Toscanini: Champion of Democracy 131

A star and more than that. Toscanini and the Media 151

MOMENTS OF A REMARKABLE LIFE 169

TIMELINE 222

ARTURO TOSCANINI, ITALIAN TITAN

Antonio Pappano

Every Italian conductor—even one like myself, born in England and brought up in America—has the spectre of Arturo Toscanini looking over his shoulder. His name alone conjures up the definition of conductorial authority and the legacy of Italian lyric theater; this is undeniable. Toscanini's temperament was so clearly Latin, so dramatic, yet he was preoccupied (maniacally so) with marrying his Mediterranean nature to a most scrupulous approach to musical execution, precision of a rare intensity. He rehearsed through repetition, virtually imprinting the music on his players—it was almost as if they were being carved into the shape he wanted. This precision was always allied to an immense sense of theater, and of history. To think that this man gave the first performances of *Pagliacci*, *La Bohème*, *La fanciulla del West* and *Turandot* is truly awe-inspiring.

We know him mainly from recordings made for NBC in the terribly dry Studio 8H. What we hear is distilled conducting, no fat, absolutely lean—the effect is electrifying but there is not a lot of tonal allure. His feverish, passionate approach to music needed a warmer environment. If you go back to the recordings he made with the Philadelphia Orchestra, or the New York Philharmonic, or the BBC Symphony, or at Salzburg with the Vienna Philharmonic, you hear a different conductor: color, allure, breath.

To accentuate the many positive attributes, I think his qualities of articulation, phrasing, style and energy, of structural clarity and balance, should appeal very much to a modern world. Toscanini put a microscope on each score he conducted. His fidelity to the score was famous. He had tremendous class, even in the way he dressed, tremendous taste. He came along at a time when orchestras had developed a lot of bad habits, the use of portamento had gone to an extreme, and "tradition" was a catch-all for sloppiness and cheap effects.

He had an important role in simplifying things, in making conductors really look at what is written in the score, and encouraging them to become the most ardent disciples of the composer. It was religion for him. Toscanini redefines the notion of pulse. He gives it an incredible, life-enhancing energy: it's so real, so wonderfully palpable in so much repertoire.

As to how we conductors should view Toscanini today, I think that to be confronted with such directness is a challenge. We're all looking to be different, searching for ways in which we can express our own personalities; but to be faced with a directness, a clarity of expression and delivery like Toscanini's, is like a gauntlet thrown down to us.

His music-making is still relevant. If one has ideas, they have to be clear to one's audience; the ideas crafted so that the audience can receive them clearly. The template for "ideas" being, of course, the score. Fidelity to the score above all.

How interesting to listen to those late recordings of his—as performances in general were getting slower, he was getting faster! The first thing that people mention about any Italian conductor is his lyrical quality, but there is far more to Toscanini. The way we perceive him has to do with propulsion, forward motion. Music that has very long paragraphs is performed in a way that always moves forward, the direction of the phrases is always fluid.

That sense of fluidity can be all the greater from a Latin temperament because of the natural fluidity of the Romance languages and their inevitable relationship to music and to the "home team" musicians. I am of Italian heritage, the challenge for me is to give warmth and generosity of sound and still keep this strong life-pulse. Toscanini has pointed the way for us.

The octogenarian Arturo Toscanini, circa 1950, described himself to a young colleague "They say I've always been the same. That's the most foolish thing that's ever been uttered about me. I've never been the same, not even from one day to the next. I've known it even if others haven't."

The statement could serve as an appropriate introduction to a reevaluation of Toscanini's gigantic position in the history of musical performance.

Toscanini had a rather amazing life: born in the provincial town of Parma, Italy, when Rossini and Berlioz were still alive, when Verdi had just completed *Don Carlos*, when Wagner was working on *Die Meistersinger* and Brahms was working on his *Deutsches Requiem*, and when Elgar, Puccini, Mahler, Debussy,

Richard Strauss, and Sibelius were between two and ten years old, he lived to see all of these composers become "classics" and to perform the music of some of them on television and record it on long-playing discs.

A rich and complicated figure was Arturo Toscanini, and let's hope that the events connected to this anniversary year will stimulate young musicians and music lovers to become acquainted with his personality and his remarkable and forever valuable recorded legacy.

MUSIC
AS A MISSION

"I love and take pride in all the works I conduct,
whether symphonic or theatrical, for...
I only conduct what I love."

A SORCERER, A MIRACLE WORKER

Toscanini and the Search for Authenticity

The secret behind La Scala's perfection is just this: it has a director, Toscanini. He insisted that every detail should be perfect: the operas are rehearsed until the executions are flawless. He doesn't just watch over the stage, but the auditorium as well: the seating area is immersed in darkness as soon as the performance begins, and no late-comers are allowed to take their seats until the act has ended. For the musician an even more admirable thing is the absolute control he has over the singers. Needless to say, the orchestra is superb, and it is interesting to note how its way of playing is typically Italian. Italians are individualists and Toscanini knows how to exploit the advantages of their nature; he especially makes sure that the wind instruments are brilliant, and this allows Toscanini to emphasize many of the passages in an Italian opera that a German conductor would sacrifice to the composition overall.

EDWARD J. DENT (1924)

Toscanini's star first began to rise when the path undertaken by the great directors of the previous generation had been completed. In many ways he crowned their work. It was a process of transformation that in just a few decades had led to the affirmation of a single director, who combined the tasks that had initially been carried out by the *maestro concertatore* and the first violin-director. This new director figure no longer had the obligation to play a keyboard instrument or the violin during the performance, but used a baton or just his hands to make himself understood by the musicians as he stood before them. This was a figure responsible for guaranteeing that the composer's wishes be respected, translating those wishes into sound before an audience. Eventually, a new professional figure emerged, one that was so capable and authoritative that it could assume full responsibility for the execution of a work, from every point of view.

Toscanini became the model *par excellence* for that figure, ever since, in 1920, he was nominated "plenipotentiary director" of the Teatro alla Scala, as well as being charged with completely reorganizing the institution's artistic, social, and financial administration. The novelty was felt by everyone, to the extent that many believed it was thanks to him that the utmost musical authority of that day and age was now, for the first time ever, a performer, and not a composer, as had been before. Toscanini had achieved that much-envied position after being the *direttore stabile* (artistic director) of three major theaters: the Teatro Regio in Turin from 1895 to 1898, the Teatro alla Scala in Milan from 1898 to 1908, the Metropolitan Opera Company in New York from 1908 to 1915. When Toscanini returned to La Scala, the situation had changed radically: in fact, in 1920 the theater had assumed a new institutional form that de facto sanctioned the end of the system based on entrepreneurial management that had characterized Italian theaters for almost three hundred years. As things stood now, Toscanini's work was not limited to curating the music; he was also responsible for the theater's calendar of events and production: it was a wholly unprecedented central position.

What happened at La Scala on April 26, 1926, at the world premiere of Giacomo Puccini's *Turandot*, which was unfinished due to the death of the composer, was the very expression of this central position. Perhaps no other premiere has ever been so closely linked to the gesture of its interpreter, in this case epitomized by the words uttered by Toscanini when he ended the performance exactly where the author had interrupted his composition: "Here the opera ends, left unfinished owing to the passing of Puccini." However, it was an undisputed fact that the conductor would in the end be the absolute protagonist of the event, even beyond the painful circumstances that had deprived him of the composer's presence. Taking advantage of his freedom to decide, Toscanini had refused to start the evening with the Fascist anthem, in spite of the fact that Mussolini was expected to attend the performance. His decision stemmed from his absolute respect for music, which for the conductor was not to be exposed to any sort of conditioning or manipulation, and it also derived from his rebelliousness when it came to official ceremonies and political events in particular. In this aspect his family imprinting was easily noticeable, as his father had set off as a volunteer with Garibaldi's 1860 military expedition, and also due to the city he had grown up in, which was pervaded in those years by a deep-seated intolerance for impositions that called into question one's freedom to do as one wished, from every point of view. These aspects were also destined to become part of the legend of Toscanini that was already taking shape. After his death in 1957, in fact, *The Etude*, a Philadelphia music magazine, published the following words:

Toscanini's father was a follower of Garibaldi, in his crusades to liberate Italy, and the young Arturo, deeply impressed by his father's stories of those days, became imbued with ideals of democracy which he defended all his life, sometimes at great cost to himself [...]

When Mussolini strangled Italy, the Fascist hymn was a mandatory part of all public programs, but Toscanini refused to play the song. When physically attacked by Fascist mobs, he remained steadfast in his refusal and carried on a personal war with dictatorship.

After the world premiere of *Turandot*, Toscanini again refused to conduct the Fascist anthem several years later, in 1931, in Bologna. On that occasion, as a consequence of his refusal he was attacked and physically injured by a group of Fascists, an incident that led to his decision to no longer conduct in Italy as long as Mussolini was in power.

However, before reasons beyond his control that had nothing to do with music ended up determining the decisions that would affect his life and his career, Toscanini's longing to be "just" a musician, still sheltered him to a great extent from the many outside influences, and could still be expressed in his mission as a performer. The truth of the matter is more complex and subtle than one might think based on the proverbial image of Toscanini as the staunch defender of what was written down in the score. The concept of loyalty to the text for Toscanini actually meant loyalty to what he believed was the composer's genuine thinking. The written page was only a reverberation of that thinking, in any case to be interpreted as long as this was done with respect for and awareness of its creator's intentions. In that way the field was open to what might even appear to be arbitrary decisions or contradictions, when he, a true son of his day and age, had no qualms about making changes that he believed were improvements to the music he was conducting. But Toscanini, in truth, could count on a reputation and authority that were

so great he could impose his point of view on anyone without too much discussion. During the New York Philharmonic Orchestra's European tour in 1930, in Paris, Toscanini conducted Ravel's *Bolero* with a tempo that the composer felt was too fast. But then it was Ravel himself who wrote to Toscanini:

Dear friend, I recently discovered that there has been a Toscanini-Ravel "affair." You must not have been aware of it either, although I've been told that it was all over the newspapers. It seems that when they applauded at the Opéra I chose not to get up to punish you for not having used the right tempo in the Bolero.
I have always felt that the composer who does not take part in the performances of his work must not receive the ovation, which must be directed only to the performer and the work, or to both. Unfortunately, I was placed in a bad—or perhaps excellent—situation at your concert, where my own absenteeism would not go by unnoticed. As I didn't want my attitude to be misunderstood, I tried turning to you, to thank you. But maliciousness lends itself to news better than the truth—don't you agree?...

And in a second letter, written a few days later, Ravel again addressed Toscanini asking him if he would be interested in conducting the world premiere of his *Piano Concerto in G*. Case closed, in other words.
The episode, which in practical terms, was an elegant step backwards by the composer, could only be explained by the fact that the conductor had become a legend, and was so wherever he went. The famous French critic Émile Vuillermoz, among other things a great promoter of the music of Debussy and Ravel, on the occasion of a later visit to Paris by Toscanini, in 1934, described him as being: "A sorcerer. A miracle worker. A being endowed by nature with exceptional fluidic power. In

the Middle Ages, such a being would have been burnt at the stake for his sorcery. Today, instead, he is recognized as the most prodigious 'sorcerer' of music ever."

Because he was surrounded by such public acclaim it should come as no surprise that the great "sorcerer of music" even succeeded in imposing his point of view on the composers themselves. There are countless instances to prove that this was so. An exchange between Toscanini and Ildebrando Pizzetti, the author of the opera *Fra Gherardo* which in 1927 was being mounted at La Scala, is an eye-opener. The topic of discussion was the measure of a note in a passage played by the trumpets: the master blamed the assistant conductor for what he felt was a written mistake in the score; but when the composer personally showed him that the note was correct Toscanini retorted that he preferred it the other way. And there is reason to believe that Pizzetti gave in to the maestro's opinion.

And there's another example as well: in a book he wrote, orchestra conductor Erich Leinsdorf, assistant conductor in Salzburg from 1934 to 1937, recalled the changes that Toscanini had made to Debussy's *La mer*. And the scores of the same composition and of the *Nocturnes*, also by Debussy, preserved in New York in the New York Philharmonic Society archives, in fact, feature several interventions by the conductor with respect to the original composition.

The conductor Ernest Ansermet has also pointed out that there are changes to some of Debussy's as well as Beethoven's scores. In some of the cases are recorded in detail the changes that were made to the instrumentation of the music he was conducting: for example, by adding a trumpet in a passage of Bedřich Smetana's *Moldava*; the reason for this was that that particular part wasn't clear enough if it was only played by trombones; or,

as documented by video footage this time, by adding a second cello to the one already included in the famous solo that begins the overture of Rossini's *William Tell*.

In the latter cases, in particular, clearly the conductor decided to make these changes for the purpose of interpreting the passage in question in the best way possible, and thus expressing precisely what he believed the composer had imagined. In other cases still, his interpretation of a score did not refute *a priori* the application of unwritten customs of execution, as long as they didn't go against the composer's intentions and the nature of the piece.

I am referring, for example, to the execution on the part of the tenor of the two notoriously high Cs in the cabaletta *Di quella pira* from Verdi's *Trovatore*: it is commonly known that the two high notes are not actually written down in the score, but, contrary to what is sometimes believed, Toscanini always accepted their execution, as can be evinced from the critical reviews of the performances of 1902 and 1925 in Milan, and of 1929 in Berlin. In yet another case, it was the director himself who openly declared that he had nothing against practices of this kind. These were his own words in a letter he wrote in 1951 to the baritone Giuseppe Valdengo, where he said that he had always accepted the singers' custom to replace with a higher note ("puntatura") the one that had originally been written in the score of the Violetta-Germont duet in the second act of *La Traviata*. He added that he preferred it to the original notes written by Verdi.

Lastly, in yet other cases, the director's intervention also concerned a change in the tonality of a piece, for example, by lowering it in order to favor its execution. Such was the case with the soprano Lotte Lehmann in the *Fidelio* performed in Salzburg in 1937 and in all likelihood with the tenor Aureliano Pertile in the *Trovatore* in Milan in 1925.

But these were not the aspects on which Toscanini's loyalty to the original composition was measured. He was convinced that to grasp the sense and the spirit of a composition it was essential to be as rigorous as possible in one's respect for the intonation, the rhythmical values, the tempo, and the colors the author had in mind, as well as the equilibrium between the various orchestra sections and between them and the voices. However, safeguarding these aspects of the work did not mean that the conductor's work was reduced to the mechanical translation of a score: quite the contrary, seeing that every commentator, from every time and every place, always praised the originality and expressive freedom of his interpretations. And so when in 1929 the German Franz Köppen in the pages of the *Berliner Börsen Zeitung* wrote that Toscanini was not a "creative" conductor, what he meant was that the maestro did not aspire to take the composer's place, like many of his fellow conductors, but rather to perform "his work from the podium" in the manner of "a religious service toward the work of art, in the spirit of its creator." Hence, it was a question of weights and measures. And indeed it was clear that Toscanini's rather numerous interventions on the scores were carried out with total respect, if compared, evidently, with the meddling of others instead, who unscrupulously misrepresented the composition and the intentions of its author. It is in this sense, then, that we are to understand his profession of humility—which for us is also a statement of intent—in a conversation he had in the home of friends, in Florence, after the last Italian concert of the European tour in 1930:

The foremost quality in a director? Humility, humility … If something does not go right, it is because I have not understood the composer. It is all my fault! Anyone who thinks that Mozart, Beethoven, Wagner, and Verdi have written music that is wrong and must be corrected is an idiot. One must study more, start over again, understand better. Those composers did not write music so that I could make a good impression. I'm the one who must help them to make a good impression, revealing them as they are, bring both myself and the orchestra close to them, as much as I possibly can, a hair's breadth away from them. The conductor does not create: the conductor executes. Humility, loyalty, clarity, unity …

A TITAN AMONG TITANS
Toscanini portrayed in Berlin in the late 1920s with the greatest conductors of that day and age: to his right, Bruno Walter, to his left, Erich Kleiber, Otto Klemperer, and Wilhelm Furtwängler.

CHARISMA ON THE PODIUM
Toscanini during the American tour with the NBC Symphony Orchestra
(April–May 1950), photographed by the cellist Emmerich Gara.
On the following pages, conducting the Wiener Philharmoniker in 1930
and again with the NBC Symphony.

*Poster for the Schubert concert
at La Scala in October 1928.*

Toscanini's Steinway piano with the portraits of his favorite composers: Giuseppe Verdi, Giacomo Puccini, Arrigo Boito, Richard Wagner; in the background, on the rear wall, Claude Debussy.

IMPRESA PIONTELLI·RHO

TEATRO ✠ REGIO
TORINO — TORINO

⌐ LETTERA O PARI ⌐

SABATO 1º Febbraio 1896, alle ore 20,30

Prima Rappresentazione
della NUÓVISSIMA Opera

LA BOHÈME

Scene da *La vie de Bohème* di *Henri Mürger*

4 Quadri

di GIUSEPPE GIACOSA e LUIGI ILLICA, *musica di* GIACOMO PUCCINI

(Proprietà G. Ricordi e C.)

PERSONAGGI

Rodolfo, poeta	Gorga Evan
Schaunard, musicista	Pini Corsi Antonio
Benoit, padrone di casa	Polonini Alessandro
Mimì	Ferrani Cesira
Parpignol	Zucchi Dante
Marcello, pittore	Wilmant Tieste
Colline, filosofo	Mazzara Michele
Alcindoro, consigliere di stato	Polonini Alessandro
Musetta	Pasini Camilla
Sergente dei doganieri	Foglia Felice

Studenti - Sartine - Borghesi - Bottegai e Bottegaie - Venditori ambulanti - Soldati - Camerieri da caffè Ragazzi - Ragazze, ecc.

Epoca: 1830 circa — a Parigi.

〜〜〜〜

Maestro Concertatore e Direttore d'Orchestra, Arturo Toscanini

Maestro sostituto e Direttore dei Cori PIETRO NEPOTI — Direttore sceno-tecnico DAVIDE FRANCHI

I scenari sono espressamente dipinti dal sigg. GHEDUZZI e GOLDINI - Il vestiario è confezionato dalla Sartoria ZAMPERONI

PALCHI: I ordine L. 45 - II ordine L. 60 - III ordine L. 45   IV ordine L. 30 - V ordine L. 15
Sedie chiuse L. 15 (oltre l'ingr.) - Posti num. di Platea L. 7,50 (oltre l'ingr.) - Posti num. di 1ª Gall. L. 6 (oltre l'ingr.)
Posti numerati di seconda Galleria L. 3 (oltre l'ingresso)
INGRESSO: Platea, Palchi e Prima Galleria L. 5 - Seconda Galleria L. 3
Loggione indistintamente L. 1,50

Torino, 1896 - Tip. Ditta G. Robbia

MUSIC'S NEW LEASE ON LIFE

Toscanini and Puccini

The central nature of the figure of the conductor, so perfectly embodied by Toscanini, ended up also reinforcing the maestro's tendency to second the composers, giving their music what many saw as being a new lease on life. What routinely happened to the works of late composers, such as Verdi and Wagner, whose interpretation had been modified over time by improper traditions, could also befall the works of career authors, like Puccini, who has left us with the most eloquent testimony of Toscanini's role in that respect. In December 1923, after a performance of *Manon Lescaut* at La Scala, the music critic of the *Corriere della Sera*, Italy's most important newspaper, had felt that changes had been made to the original composition of the opera. Puccini replied to him in a letter he wrote to the newspaper:

My Manon *is exactly the same opera that it was thirty years ago, only now it has been directed... by Arturo Toscanini, who brought its composer the rare joy of hearing his own music so illuminated with a brightness which he only dreamt about at the moment he was composing it, and which he has never heard this way, until now. For way too long it has been the custom in Italy to perform the standard repertory operas, especially those that have resisted the ravages of time and countless inadequate or musically unfaithful productions, after they receive only a single orchestra rehearsal, and almost none at all for the staging. Then this worthless production goes before the public, once again deformed by these horrible abuses which have become encrusted through the poor habits and tastes of untalented singers and conductors.*

But with Toscanini, we are all enflamed by the marvelous skill with which he takes a score, like when a sculptor takes a chisel in his hand and clears away all the filth which had accumulated on the music and brings it back to its pristine, original state, only then revealing the composer's true musical intention to the public. Now the old opera seems brand new, and the public says: it has become something entirely different. No, it is simply the same one, rejuvenated by the greatest performer that musical art can boast of. […] set designers and musicians and singers enthusiastically do all they can, and this huge amount of energy led and brought to life by Toscanini achieves such results that, like last night, Manon appears to be a new opera, and I myself felt I was thirty years younger; and upon leaving the Scala I forgot that I was stepping down from the stage and not from the box like three decades ago […].

One year later, Puccini passed away in Brussels. Toscanini received the news during a rehearsal, which he abruptly interrupted so that he could go to his dressing room and be by himself to mourn his loss. It would be up to him to conduct the composer's last work, *Turandot*, which remained fatefully unfinished. In the past, Toscanini had directed the world premieres of two other works by Puccini: *La bohème*, in 1896, and *La fanciulla del West*, on December 10, 1910, the most important premiere opera conducted by Toscanini during his period at the Metropolitan. The conductor, as was customary for him and in agreement with the composer, had also collaborated in determining several aspects of the final version of the opera, especially with regard to its orchestration.

Toscanini's personal relationship with Puccini had begun midway through the previous decade, at first when he directed *Manon Lescaut* in Pisa, and later with the world premiere of *La bohème* in Turin in 1896. At first, Puccini was not at all eager to let Toscanini be the first to conduct his opus: he was not happy about its debuting in Turin, and he would have preferred another conductor, specifically the renowned Leopoldo Mugnone, who a few years earlier had conducted the premiere of Mascagni's *Cavalleria rusticana*.

In a letter Puccini wrote he described Toscanini as a "difficult customer," probably in reference to his harsh personality and to the fact that he was a real stickler when it came to work. But then, when he saw with his own eyes the commitment, devotion, and the quality of the director's work in honing the opera, he could only express his great appreciation and gratitude. And from that moment onwards, in spite of some highs and lows in their relationship, Puccini would always emphasize Toscanini's kindness and generosity toward him.

After *La bohème* came *La fanciulla del West*. Puccini's decision to look to California, which for him was the next frontier of exoticism after the Japanese setting of *Madama Butterfly*, unquestionably had a lot to do with the appeal of a rich and growing market such as that of the United States. And after all, the example set by the general director of the theater, Gatti-Casazza, and by Toscanini, in addition to that set by an entire legion of Italian singers who by that time were settling in the United States, was full proof of how the decision might be the right one.

The choice of *The Girl of the Golden West*, the play that the Californian director and producer David Belasco had directed with great success in New York in 1905, as the plot of Puccini's new opera, meant taking a huge risk, however, as in the United States the performance was also going to be judged by some critics on the plausibility of its setting. It could not have been otherwise, as the world of the gold diggers in the Cloudy Mountains of California in the mid-nineteenth century was as foreign to Puccini's world as Butterfly's Japan or Turandot's China.

Nonetheless, Puccini had no trouble releasing statements for the press in which he assured everyone that he had carried out so much research into the theme of the "California Gold Rush" and its protagonists that he was sure to have expressed in his opera the truest and most genuine spirit of the American people. It was, of course, an element of the communications strategy set in motion by the Metropolitan, which overcame any doubts that might have arisen about the depiction of the Old West. There were high expectations for Puccini's new opera dedicated to America and to its legends, tickets quickly sold out, and there was heavy traffic in the streets around the theater. The show was a smash hit, with dozens of curtain calls.

The production was sumptuous, with a fine cast, whose actors and actresses—Emmy Destinn (Minnie), Enrico Caruso (Dick Johnson), Pasquale Amato (Jack Rance)—were immortalized in a famous series of pictures taken of them in their costumes.

Rehearsals for La fanciulla del West *as seen by an exceptional illustrator, the tenor Enrico Caruso. In addition to the other characters, at the back of the stage, looking out from a half-open door, is the general director of the theater, Giulio Gatti-Casazza.*

A FRUITFUL COLLABORATION
*In the company of Puccini on the occasion
of the French premiere of* Manon Lescaut,
Paris 1910.

Posters by the Ricordi publishing house dedicated to La Bohème (Alfred Hohenstein) and Turandot (Leopoldo Metlicovitz), both of which were conducted by Toscanini for the world premiere in Turin in 1896, and in Milan in 1926.

On the opposite page, poster by the Ricordi publishing house for Puccini's La fanciulla del West, *a live premiere performance by Toscanini at the Metropolitan Opera House in New York in 1910.*
Above, from left to right, the general director of the Metropolitan Opera Giulio Gatti-Casazza, the playwright David Belasco, Arturo Toscanini, and Giacomo Puccini in New York in 1910 for the debut of La fanciulla del West.

THE WEST GOES ON STAGE
Stage photograph of the third act of
La fanciulla del West *at the moment
when it must be decided whether the
main character should be sentenced
to death. At the center: Enrico Caruso
(Dick Johnson) and Emmy Destinn
(Minnie); to the right, in the foreground:
Pasquale Amato (Jack Rance).
On the following pages, the two main
characters in costume.*

WAGNER'S INFLUENCE

Toscanini and the "Greatest Composer of the Century"

Among operas, I value those of Verdi and Wagner above all. It is difficult to state a preference for one of Wagner's operas. I have noticed that if I am conducting one or another of Wagner's operas, or playing it at the piano, whichever one it happens to be takes possession of my heart. And yet, every time I glance at the score of Parsifal, *I say to myself: This is the sublime one. In Verdi's operas, I appreciate not only the richness of the melodies but also the effective and sure power of the musical drama. When I conduct* Falstaff *at Busseto I think about the possibility of a Verdian Bayreuth, along the lines of Wagner's Festspielhaus. These two masters are the real representatives of German and Italian national music.*

A.T. (1932)

In many respects Toscanini's relationship with music was the fruit of the relationship he had with Wagner's music. The greatest musician of the century, according to the maestro's own words, hence, the greatest ever, given the absolute preponderance of nineteenth-century composers in his repertoire. And this was a musician who, as a German newspaper once stated, usually conducted only works by the composers he liked.

Toscanini's encounter with Wagner's music had the effect of an early revelation on the conductor, when, still a student at Parma's Royal School of Music, he heard the overture of the *Tannhäuser* during a concert of the local Quartet Society. "I was completely awe-struck," he revealed many years later, remembering that his cello teacher made him study several passages of the overture, which had at first seemed unsurmountable to him. But a few years later, as he got closer to earning his diploma, the young cello player ended up playing with the orchestra of the Teatro Regio di Parma, which was performing *Lohengrin*:

In 1884 Parma was the first Italian city in which Lohengrin was performed, after its success at Bologna and its fiasco at Milan. I was in the orchestra. I had then the first true, great, sublime revelation of Wagner's genius. At the first rehearsal and from the very beginning the prelude gave me magic supernatural impressions, with its divine harmonies which revealed to me an entire new world, a world that no one dreamed existed, before it was discovered by the supernatural mind of Wagner.

For no other composer would Toscanini have reserved such expressions of sincere and deferent enthusiasm: "Here is the tomb of the greatest composer of the century!" he wrote in 1899 to his brother-in-law, the violinist Enrico Polo, in a postcard that showed Wagner's grave in Wahnfried. This does not mean, to be sure, that Toscanini's preference for the German maestro was so great that it should preclude him from other elective affinities.

In the summer of 1905, during a vacation in the Alps, he climbed up Mont Blanc, the highest peak in Italy: once again Enrico Polo received a postcard filled with Toscanini's enthusiasm, his near inebriation before such stunning heights, both in real and metaphorical terms. "We climbed Mont Blanc. Dante, Beethoven, Wagner! We quiver with enthusiasm." And then: "Every time I stand upon the podium and am about to begin conducting Beethoven I feel as though I were at the foot of a huge mountain and were getting ready to climb it."

These were not words and images of circum-stance: it was Toscanini's opinion about the maestro from Bonn, an opinion he had nurtured early on when he was a student, and that he was to preserve for the rest of his life. It was an opinion that always involved the feeling and the fear that he was supposed to express something that wasn't humanly possible to express, like when, hard at work on the "Adagio" of the *Ninth Symphony*, he confessed to his friend Anna Mainardi that at times he felt so close to the Elysian Fields, to Paradise, that he could have conducted it with his eyes closed.

Only later would he add another composer to Wagner and Beethoven, that is, Verdi, for whose last opera, *Falstaff*, he would develop such a definite preference that he, a die-hard Wagnerian, even preferred it to the *Meistersinger*: "*Meistersinger* is a magnificent work; but *Falstaff* is really something else," he confessed during a conversation on a train. And then, after comparing Rossini's *Barber of Seville* with Mozart's *The Marriage of Figaro*, he added: "I think that the same difference exists, after all, between *Falstaff*, which is an absolute masterpiece, and the *Meistersinger*, an outstanding work by Wagner. Just think for a moment how many musical means—beautiful ones, of course—Wagner must make use of to describe what nighttime was like in Nuremberg. And look how Verdi gets a similarly startling effect from just *three notes*."

Hence, Wagner, Beethoven, and Verdi, and many, many others, of course, especially in the grandiose opera and symphonic repertoire from the late-eighteenth to the early-twentieth centuries. But always under the influence of Wagner, a point of reference so inexorable that Toscanini was willing to stand up in person not just to defend the right to perform his favorite composer's music, but also to proclaim, during the rather sensitive period of World War I, the independence of music in general from all outside influences.

Indeed, in 1916, in a climate marked by strong anti-German sentiment in Italy, the conductor was fiercely attacked by a newspaper for having included Wagner's music in a concert program. The fact was reported in a satirical periodical published in Turin, whose headline was: *L'ultima vittoria di Toscanini* (Toscanini's Last Victory):

A newspaper in Turin, given that the maestro Toscanini had included a piece by Wagner in his concert at the Teatro Regio, published some heavily critical articles. When faced with this, Toscanini thought it best that he "direct," if not a composition for orchestra, then a letter to the newspaper: he then ended up going to the newspaper and remonstrating with the "heartless" editorial staff. If Orpheus succeeded in taming the beasts with one instrument, what then might a famous orchestra conductor be capable of doing? And in the end, the newspaper changed its tune, ceasing its hostility toward Wagner. [...]

Aside from this incident, we cannot overlook the fact that many of the most significant phases in the conductor's career were in the name of the German composer: in 1895 Toscanini made his debut as *direttore stabile* (artistic director) of Turin's Teatro Regio with *Die Götterdämmerung*; in 1898 he assumed the directorship of the Teatro alla Scala in Milan, where he conducted *Die Meistersinger von Nürnberg*; on March 20, 1948, in New York at NBC headquarters, he conducted one of the first concerts in the world recorded by a television station, with a program entirely dedicated to Wagner; and two of the farewell concerts he conducted, on September 19, 1952 and April 4, 1954, at Carnegie Hall and at La Scala, respectively, with the NBC Symphony Orchestra, were also influenced by Wagner. Not to mention Toscanini's efforts to make the German

composer's works better known in Italy by promoting various national premiere concerts.

But the most significant event was almost certainly the maestro's participation at the Bayreuth Festival, the first non-German-school conductor invited to conduct in the temple consecrated to the worship of Wagner. For Toscanini it was the crowning of an aspiration that had begun to develop way back in 1884, when, as a young student, he discovered the music composed by the artist who was to become his favorite composer. It was a dream come true, and perhaps a fitting tribute, as testified by the fact that Toscanini never accepted payment for his participation at the Festival. Rather, it was a dream and a tribute that grew within a specific sphere, the Italian one, where the young Toscanini had done his training, in which the music and the figure of the Leipzig composer had assumed an increasingly dominant position.

After the Italian première of *Lohengrin*, in Bologna in 1871, the name Wagner grew more and more present on Italian theater playbills, and was used as a benchmark for all the new operas, including Verdi's. So it should come as no surprise that the German composer's name and his music represented a legend also for the Italian musicians who were being trained in the second half of the nineteenth century. Wagner, more than Verdi and the other Italian and foreign composers, was the name most in vogue in Italy's musical culture at the turn of the century, and it represented for everyone—supporters and adversaries—the model to compare oneself with.

Toscanini was a good example of this growing trend. In 1929, on the occasion of the Scala's triumphant tour in Vienna, the newspaper

Neue Freie Presse printed a declaration in which the conductor, to show his love and admiration for Wagner, confessed that he had called his son "Walter after the hero of the *Meistersinger*": the young man in love, the noble knight Walther von Stolzing. Indeed, the maestro's son Walter was born in March 1898, just a few months before Toscanini's debut at La Scala, where he performed that very work: *Die Meistersinger*.

It was in that perfect harmony between private sphere and artistic dimension that Toscanini worked on his participation at the Bayreuth Festival. He had been there as a member of the public many years before, in July 1899, when he had attended performances of *Die Meistersinger*, directed by Hans Richter, and *Parsifal*, which in those days was exclusively performed in Bayreuth, conducted by Franz von Fischer, and especially the whole tetralogy, *Der Ring des Nibelungen*, conducted by Siegfried Wagner, the composer's son.

Siegfried's and Arturo's paths were destined to cross again: two years later, in January 1901 at La Scala, Siegfried attended the production of *Tristan und Isolde* conducted by Toscanini, with stage designs by the famous painter and set designer Mariano Fortuny.

Siegfried was deeply moved by the experience—which was about both the value of music and the stage design: he was active not just as an orchestra conductor, but as a theater director, too—and very soon he became a fervent admirer of Toscanini and of his "holistic" way of conceiving the opera. Evidence of this can be found in the letter that Cosima Liszt—the composer's widow, Siegfried's mother, and at the time in charge of the Bayreuth Festival—sent to Toscanini on January 18:

My son has given me an account of the performance of Tristan *which he attended in Milan, and he has told me so many good things about it that I take upon myself the duty of expressing to you the contentment I feel in knowing that a work of such great difficulty has been performed with care on a foreign stage.*

My son has insisted on the minutious zeal you have brought to the study of the orchestra and on the excellent results achieved because of this zeal, combined with your great skill as Kapellmeister. He has also told me that the singers have a perfect grasp of their roles and that they performed with warmth and enthusiasm.

Lastly, he has spoken to me with great satisfaction about the stage setting due to the talent of Mr. Fortuny. And—above all—he has noted the close attention and the general animation of the public.

All these indications of your respect towards and instinct for the incomparable work to which you have dedicated yourself with so much ardor made my son very happy to have been a witness, and at a distance I join his satisfaction [...]

After that experience, Siegfried began thinking about how he could get Toscanini to Bayreuth. It would have been a way to reinvigorate the Wagnerian tradition, freeing it from the burden of a musical and theatrical practice that had by then become obsolete, as well as from the many musical and extra-musical approximations and encrustations that over the decades had distorted the composer's artistic thinking. The potential novelty represented by the Italian director also consisted in the way he dealt with the score and its staging: in his approach his implacable analytical rigor was combined with a pragmatic and non-ideological attitude, according to the Italian musical and theatrical tradition.

Siegfried's plan failed, at first, because of the resistance of both the Wagner family and the Festival's artistic staff. Only many years later, in 1929, when Toscanini's international acclaim had reached a peak, did Siegfried manage to overcome every obstacle, inviting the Italian maestro to come the following year, well aware of the explosive effect of having a non-German-school conductor in the temple consecrated to the worship of his father, for the first time after over five decades since its inauguration. Although it was probably the effect Siegfried wanted, it was unexpected by many, as Herbert von Karajan, twenty at the time, recalls:

In Bayreuth, as soon as Toscanini arrived, I realized what "precision" meant to him. It was an unlikely precision—in other words, not mechanical, but simply a spiritual force that emanated from the rigor of the music taken literally and that subordinated everything. It was almost a revolution, [...] the orchestra was together, the chorus was together, the orchestra was together with the chorus ... something that was rather rare in those days! The standards were mostly poor. I remember one of the first things he said when the singers began shouting, as they are often forced to when they interpret Wagner, was: "No, no, no nix Bayreuth, Café Chantant!" and he taught them to sing low, which produced magnificent results, especially considering the Tannhäuser, *which has so many grandiose ensembles.*

The chronicles and memories of those who were there to experience it have left for us descriptions of the astonishing impact that Toscanini's arrival had on the Festival. After a first approach the conductor refused to continue rehearsing until all the musicians, which he was not satisfied with, had been replaced. The situation is well illustrated in a cartoon published in Germany at the time, which portrayed Toscanini turning his back to the podium with the score on it and covering his ears while shouting: "no, no, no, no!" This was one frequent example of Toscanini's constant dissatisfaction with the way anyone, first and foremost himself, tried to translate into sound the thoughts the composer had written down in the score. The scene was repeated wherever he was invited to conduct, and it no doubt contributed to the many anecdotes that were said to be true about Toscanini.

In Bayreuth, in particular, besides the poor level of some of the musicians, Toscanini found the lack of homogeneity within the various sections of the orchestra to be totally unacceptable. It was, in truth, an almost inevitable consequence for a company that did not perform together on a regular basis, comprised of musicians who came from other orchestras and who only played together for the Festival; but Toscanini was not a man willing to make compromises when it came to music, even less so when it involved Wagner in Bayreuth. For this reason, the same treatment he reserved for the orchestra was also reserved for the scores, in which each time Toscanini toiled to clean up all the errors and the variants that over decades of more or less expert performances he believed had been added to the original score. Such episodes also became part of the repertoire of anecdotes told about the maestro, confirming a sort of notoriety that is truly unimaginable today, and that went well beyond the globalized sphere of music lovers.

For instance, a few months after Toscanini's death in 1957, a popular weekly comic magazine published in Belgium and France, *Tintin* ("Le journal des jeunes de 7 à 77 ans"), featured the illustrated story of his life. One of the episodes describes how Toscanini brought a rehearsal of *Die Götterdämmerung* to a halt, violently accusing the orchestra members of having mistaken one of the notes: "Arrêtez!... Arrêtez!... C'est une honte!... Bandits!..." (Stop, stop, this is shameful, you bandits!) When told by the musicians that the note was actually written in the passages they were playing, Toscanini interrupted the rehearsal until he succeeded in demonstrating, after checking Wagner's original score, that the note had been incorrectly transcribed, and that he had been right all along... I don't know how much of this is true and how much of it is invented, but no doubt, whatever the case may be, the story was so plausible it has come to represent one of the most typical traits of Toscanini's personality, and his conception of the relationship between the person interpreting the music and its composer.

The same treatment was always reserved for the singers, with some of whom, as they traveled around the world, he had arguments that have never been forgotten. In Bayreuth, in particular, when Toscanini, with a taste for paradox, asked the singers to set aside the hard, self-important style of the Festival to instead embrace that of the *Café-chantant*, his goal was to restore greater fluidity to the vocal style in the rendering of the melodic lines, out of respect, among other things, for what Wagner himself—who had been a great admirer of Italian singing style—had always supported. The attention toward the development of the melody and all its structural prerogatives, in Wagner as in all the other composers whose works he conducted, for Toscanini assumed a value that went beyond the specific area of the voices, to instead also involve the orchestra, which he always asked to "sing" the music. And indeed, during rehearsals he might himself sing what he wanted the players to perform, rather than waste time explaining. He asked the orchestra to play with the same flow and natural breathing that is required

of singing. French director Désiré-Émile Inghelbrecht tells of having attended a rehearsal of Debussy's *La mer* in which Toscanini expected the melody to always be clearly perceived. It was not a case, Inghelbrecht continued, of a typically Italian bias, as some of his fellow conductors believed, but of the need to make evident to the public the plot of the discourse, accompanying it from bar to bar, fluidly, and not mechanically or affectedly. This is yet another concept that harkens back to Wagner himself, when in 1869 he theorized a melody that had a proper structural function.

In the end, Toscanini's Wagner was the result of an interpretation based on clarity and precision that was so unusual as to disorient many of those who were used to the Late-Romantic or early twentieth-century version of Bayreuth. The feeling was that one was hearing and seeing a different Wagner: while for some it was a betrayal, for others it was a revelation. The orchestra conductor Hans Schmidt-Isserstedt, for instance, after complaining about a first act of *Tristan und Isolde* that was even too slow and precise, remarked: "The second act: another world! I never again heard it performed as beautifully as that time—as flowing. It was almost like hearing an Italian melody... and then came the third act, grandiose, ecstatic, and completely free."

The feeling of finding oneself before the musical regeneration of Wagner was normally perceived also outside the Bayreuth experience. Years before, after attending Toscanini's *Tristan* in New York, *Telegraph* critic Algernon St. John-Brenon wrote: "There may be a Teutonic way of interpreting *Tristan und Isolde*. There may be a delicatessen way. But Mr. Toscanini's is the Wagnerian way." And again in New York, many years later, when Toscanini had settled in the city, *New York Herald Tribune* critic Lawrence Gilman described the so-called *Brünnhilde's Immolation* from the *Götterdämmerung* directed by the Italian maestro as an absolute "re-creation" in Wagner's name:

When Toscanini plays [...] the opera's fiery epilogue, while the orchestra exults and mourns and prophesizes and turns the heavens into sacrifical flame, we are aware beyond doubt or adventure that we have heard the living voice of Wagner. And we tell ourselves, in wonderment, 'But this is not the Götterdämmerung *we knew!' It is not, indeed. Yet the conviction persists that it is the* Götterdämmerung Wagner *knew—rather the* Götterdämmerung *that he conceived. And this is true of all the music by Wagner that Toscanini plays.*

At the time that Gilman wrote these words, probably in the late 1930s, Toscanini had not conducted an opera in a theater for several years, having decided in 1937, after his last participation in the Salzburg Festival, that he no longer wanted to be burdened with the task of mounting a theater performance. For the maestro the effort to do so was even more exhausting because of his need to control every single aspect of the production.

Thus, the two seasons spent in Bayreuth can be considered among the last during which Toscanini conducted Wagner's works in a theater: *Tannhäuser* and *Tristan und Isolde* in 1930, *Tannhäuser* and *Parsifal* again in 1931. But the event that undoubtedly influenced Toscanini's experience over the course of the two seasons and, at least in part, his decision to turn down the invitation for the following years, was the death of Siegfried Wagner,

during the Festival itself, on August 4, 1930, a few months after the death of his mother, Cosima.

The loss of the reassuring presence of the person who had wanted him, even against the wishes of the most conservative faction at Bayreuth, also meant losing any guarantee of his being able to hold on to the preeminent position he had earned from the time of his arrival in the German city. The feeling that he was being given less importance than Wilhelm Furtwängler, who was much loved, and who had been hired for the 1931 season as "principal director" of the Festival, as well as his aversion to several choices concerning the staging of *Parsifal*, were behind Toscanini's reasons for distancing himself from Bayreuth.

To these would be added, after Hitler's rise to power in 1933, his firm opposition to the policy of discrimination toward Jewish musicians. It was an aversion that peaked when he, along with other signatories, sent from New York a cable to Hitler challenging the persecutions of Jewish musicians. The cable was published by several newspapers. Fifteen-year-old Friedelind Wagner—daughter of Siegfried and Winifred—was a witness to the effects of those words, as she had overheard a phone call between her mother and Hitler, during which it was decided that the Chancellor would send Toscanini a telegram and then a letter inviting him to return to Bayreuth.

Friedelind advised her mother that this was not the way she should proceed, as she was convinced that Hitler's invitation would have had the opposite effect on Toscanini. But it was all to no avail. Winifred, in fact, a staunch supporter of the Nazis but also a sincere admirer of Toscanini, thought it would be a good idea to send the maestro a telegram from Berlin on April 3, 1933 announcing Hitler's letter:

German government true lover of art and music highly esteems you as conductor of Bayreuth Festivals stop Letter from chancellor assuring you of welcome on the way to you heaps of loving greetings.

Toscanini waited to reply until late in April, first to Hitler, in a mild and interlocutory tone, almost as though he were waiting to see what the developments might be; and then, more resolutely, to Winifred:

The sorrowful events that wounded my human and artistic feelings have not yet undergone any change, contrary to all my hopes. Thus it is my duty today to break the silence I had imposed on myself for two months and to let you know that for my peace of mind, for yours, and for everyone's, it is better not to think about my coming to Bayreuth.
With unchangeable friendship (and affection) for the house of Wagner...

A trace of that sincere affection was to remain in the maestro's personal contacts with some of the members of the family and in the tribute he paid to his deceased friend, Siegfried, when he conducted, at the 1939 Lucerne Festival in Switzerland, the *Idyll* from *Siegfried* in Tribschen Villa, the very spot where the piece had been performed for the first time in 1870 by the composer himself on the occasion of his son's birth.

The Bayreuth Festspielhaus, the theater reserved for Wagner's works, inaugurated in 1876, in a period photograph.

On page 56, Toscanini in Bayreuth with Siegfried, Richard Wagner's son.

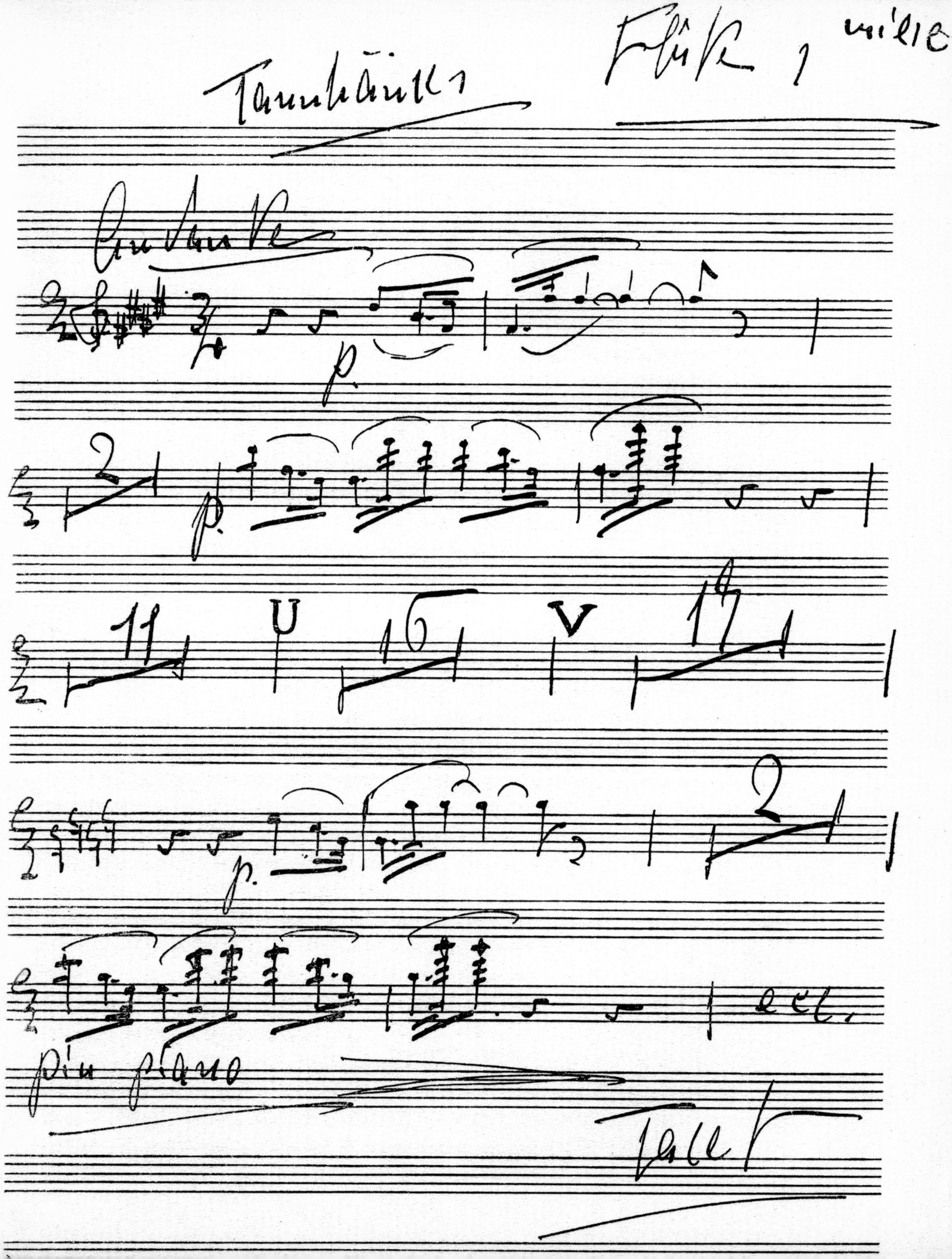
Tannhäuser
Flöte 1
Andante
p.
U
V
p.
ecc.
più piano

On the opposite page, handwritten note by Toscanini with several measures for the flute in the
overture of Wagner's Tannhäuser.
Above, postcard sent by Toscanini in 1899 while visiting Wagner's grave to his brother-in-law,
the violinist Enrico Polo. Toscanini's words were: "Here is the tomb of the greatest musician of the
century!"

WITH SIEGFRIED WAGNER: ESTEEM AND FRIENDSHIP

Above, letter written by Siegfried Wagner, February 1929: "Dear Maestro Toscanini, we sincerely thank you for your kind telegram: we are happy that you wish to come here!" Just over a year later, Toscanini would make his debut in Bayreuth. Siegfried apologized for his Italian, which is "impossible, I have never even held an Italian grammar book! I learned the language by conversing with porters, butlers, and gardeners!"

On the following page, with Siegfried Wagner in Bayreuth to mount Tristan und Isolde *in 1930. Between them, in the middle, E. Riede and E. Faltis, members of the festival's artistic staff.*

S.Wagner · Dr.A.Toscanini

S.Wagner E.Rıede E.Fallis Dr.A.Toscanini

THE FIRST NON-GERMAN CONDUCTOR ON THE PODIUM IN BAYREUTH
On the opposite page, Toscanini in the mystical gulf of Festspielhaus; above, with several of the performers in Tristan und Isolde, *1930. To his left, the two main characters: the soprano Nanny Larsén-Todsen and the tenor Lauritz Melchior.*

In 1939, during the Lucerne Festival in Switzerland, Toscanini conducts Richard Wagner's Siegfried Idyll *in the villa of Tribschen, in tribute to the composer's son, Siegfried, who died in 1930. The piece had been performed in the same place for the first time under the composer's direction in 1870, for his son's birth.*

73

R · WAGNER

1813 – 1913

G · VERDI

RICORDO DEL CENTENARIO DELLA LORO NASCITA

Stabilimento Tipo-Litografico Pellas, Luigi Chiti, successore, Firenze.

Augusto Ferraresi - Editore - SS. Apostoli, 10, Firenze.

BUSSETO AKIN TO BAYREUTH

Toscanini for Verdi

Toscanini's relationship with Verdi was also to some extent influenced by his preference for Wagner, as was natural during a period when, even in Italy, the German composer's music was considered by many to be the absolute benchmark. As for Verdi, from midway through the century the critics had begun, at first sporadically, then more and more frequently, to judge each of his works in light of the Wagnerian conception of musical theater. From *Aida* onwards, and especially as concerns the last two operas, *Otello* and *Falstaff*, the comparison would be so obsessive that it would enrage the composer:

What clowns you are!! And you want to talk to me about harmony?! There isn't an inkling of Wagner here!! On the contrary, if one really wanted to listen and understand they would find the exact opposite ... quite the opposite [...] Whatever is the meaning of these schools, these biased ideas concerning the singing, the harmony, Germanisms, Italianisms, Wagnerisms, etc. etc.? There is something more in music ... there is music! ... The public should not be concerned with the means the artists use, it should not be concerned with schools ... If the music is good then it should applaud. If it isn't, it should boo ... And that is all. Music is universal. Imbeciles and pedants have wanted to discover, and invent, schools, systems!!! ... I would like the public's opinion to rise up, and not judge based on the miserable views of the Journalists, the Maestros, and the Piano-Players, but based on its own impressions instead!*

The fact is that afterwards—Verdi's tirade took place in 1872, when *Aida* had recently been performed—Wagner's name would be associated with the Italian composer's until the end of his days. And at the time of Verdi's death, in 1901, the best Italian critics and musicians of the newest generations were all, with just a few exceptions, classified as "Wagnerians."

In such a situation it wasn't surprising that only the last works by the Italian composer—the ones that, whether rightly or wrongly, were likened to those of the German composer—were considered truly worthy of attention and appreciation. Toscanini participated in that widespread sentiment, and in many ways he stuck to his beliefs until the very end, to the extent that, with the exception of *Un ballo in maschera* and *Traviata*, his only and most famous, complete recordings of Verdi's operas were in fact *Aida*, *Otello*, and his beloved *Falstaff*.

It was precisely this fact, nevertheless, that conveyed a truly exceptional value to the "revival" of the *Trovatore* at La Scala in 1902: an opera that many at the time believed was obsolete and vulgar, and in any case no longer suited to a great theater like La Scala where, in fact, it hadn't been performed in over two decades.

Many people indeed saw the event as the date symbolizing the beginning of a renaissance of the entire Verdi repertoire that was to take place in the second half of the twentieth century. I believe that Toscanini, even beyond the episode linked to the *Trovatore*, did feel the need for an ongoing intiative dedicated to Verdi's works, championing the idea that Busseto, Verdi's birthplace, could be for the composer what Bayreuth was for Wagner—a place dedicated to the staging and artistic conservation of all of Verdi's works.

The hypothesis became more explicit in 1913, when Toscanini, then conductor at the Metropolitan, accepted the task of overseeing the choice of the music for the celebration of the centennial of Verdi's birth, to be held in Busseto. A curious fact: at the same time as the events in Busseto, other celebrations for the centennial were being held a few dozen miles away, in Parma, under the directorship of Cleofonte Campanini, an internationally acclaimed conductor, who was also born in Parma. At the time, Campanini was the conductor and general manager of the Chicago Opera Association, after having with great success conducted the Manhattan Opera in New York in previous years.

The celebrations in Busseto were more modest with respect to what could be organized in Parma. Nonetheless, thanks to Toscanini's presence and prestige, it was possible to mount two high-level productions: *La traviata* and *Falstaff*, that is to say, two of Verdi works that, owing to the colloquial style that distinguishes them, were best suited to the theater's small size. The two productions, which were carefully conceived and developed from every point of view, took place on September 20 and 21, with several world-class performers whom Toscanini had conducted on more than one occasion over the years, in the United States as well: they were the soprano Lucrezia Bori, the baritone Pasquale Amato, and the tenor Edoardo Garbin.

It was a huge success, but the proposal to transform Busseto into Bayreuth for Verdi would forever be just a pipe dream. Toscanini returned to Busseto in 1926, however, after he had long been gone from the Metropolitan and been back to La Scala for the twenty-fifth anniversary of Verdi's death.

He again chose *Falstaff*, the Verdi opera that was dearest and most congenial to him. The baritone Mariano Stabile performed the lead role, and the character of the Elizabethan knight was to become his speciality. Once again, the small size of the Busseto theater proved to be remarkably suited to the perception of the subtlety of Verdi's score, and to the perfect balance between the orchestra and the voices, for Toscanini, an indispensable requisite for every interpretation if it was to be an accurate one. On that occasion, according to all those who had the good fortune to attend, he conducted one of the most memorable performances ever of Verdi's opera.

When, years later, Toscanini conducted *Falstaff* in Berlin during the La Scala ensemble's triumphant 1929 tour, the critic Franz Köppen wrote that for him there were "no schools nor movements, and not even national restrictions," which was why he was "equally great as a loyal interpreter of Verdi as he was of Wagner." And yet, paradoxically, for Toscanini it was harder to direct for an Italian public a Verdi opera interpreted in his own way, than a Wagner opera cleansed of the Bayreuth tradition.

This should come as no surprise, as Toscanini's loyalty to Wagner consisted in exalting certain aspects that were closer to the conception of Italian opera, and that in the Wagnerian tradition of the recent decades had been lost. Whereas for the German public this came as a surprise, for others it was a revelation; for the Italian audience it obviously represented an easy way to approach the Leipzig composer's music.

In Verdi's case, instead, the loyalty to the composer's intentions had already been dissolved in the late nineteenth century owing to the effect of the new trends in the work of the latest generation of Italian composers, and to the massive importation from abroad of works that fulfilled different traditions. Toscanini, nonetheless, belonged to a generation that had formed while Verdi was still alive, and had had direct contact with him personally as well as with the performers he had trained. And he had received directly from the composer certain concepts that he was to keep in mind. In a letter written in 1871, in which he complained of the total misunderstanding of his intentions by the famous conductor Angelo Mariani in a passage from the *Forza del destino*, Verdi penned several words that Toscanini would no doubt have subscribed to:

[…] I want only one creator, and I demand that what is written is followed […]. I often read in the papers about effects that the composer never could have thought of; but for my part, I have never found such a thing. […] Neither Singers nor Conductors are allowed to create […].

And the few times Toscanini had the chance to mention doubts about his interpretation to Verdi directly, or to ask him to settle controversies that had arisen with the singers, the composer always said he was right. Such as when, during the rehearsals for *Otello* at La Scala in 1900, a dispute arose between Toscanini and the famous Francesco Tamagno concerning the tempo in one passage of the last act. The tenor, who in 1887 had sung the very first performance of the opera, said that Verdi himself had taught him the part that way; Toscanini, instead, who had also been present at the premiere as cellist, remembered things differently. So the two of them went to see the elderly composer, who said that Toscanini was right, complimenting him for the remarkable accuracy of his memory. Tamagno had no choice but to leave, grumbling that composers and conductors had the dreadful habit of always changing their minds.

On page 74, celebratory print of the centennial of the births of Wagner and Verdi, 1913.

27 Febbraio 1901.

Largo Cairoli.

MILAN AND TOSCANINI ACCOMPANY VERDI TO HIS FINAL RESTING PLACE
The procession for the transfer of the bodies of Giuseppe Verdi and his wife Giuseppina Strepponi from the Cimitero Monumentale to the Casa di Riposo per Musicisti that Verdi himself had built, Milan, February 27, 1901. On the opposite page, at the Cimitero Monumentale Toscanini conducts the chorus "Va' pensiero" from Verdi's Nabucco.

On the previous page, the Teatro Verdi in Busseto
in an early twentieth-century postcard.

Opposite, the inauguration of the monument
to Verdi in Busseto during the 1913 celebrations
for the centennial of the composer's birth.
At the center, under the name "Verdi," Toscanini's
children (Wanda, Walter, and Wally), and his wife
Carla. In the background to the right, the Spanish
soprano Lucrezia Bori, the star of the operas that
Toscanini was conducting in the Busseto theater
on that occasion.

HOMAGE TO VERDI'S BIRTHPLACE
Toscanini with the performers of Falstaff visiting Verdi's birthplace to commemorate the twenty-fifth anniversary of the composer's death, Busseto 1926.

On the following pages, the poster for the theater season directed by Toscanini in Busseto to celebrate the centennial of the birth of Verdi, and the general poster for the celebrations, created by the illustrator Leopoldo Metlicovitz.

Busseto - Teatro Verdi

1813-1913

Primo Centenario della nascita di GIUSEPPE VERDI

STAGIONE D'AUTUNNO 1913

— Si rappresenteranno le Opere —

LA TRAVIATA

Libretto in 3 atti di FRANCESCO MARIA PIAVE

FALSTAFF

Commedia lirica in 3 atti di ARRIGO BOITO

Musica di GIUSEPPE VERDI

ELENCO ARTISTICO PER ORDINE ALFABETICO

Signore: GISELLA ADORNI - LUCREZIA BORI - LINDA CANNETTI - GUERRINA FABBRI - ADELE PONZANO.
Signori: PASQUALE AMATO - ANGELO BADÀ - VINCENZO BETTONI - LUIGI BOLPAGNI - EDOARDO GARBIN - GIUSEPPE GIARDINI - ANDREA ORLANDI - GIORDANO PALTRINIERI - EMILIO PINESCHI.

Maestro Concertatore - Direttore d'Orchestra: ARTURO TOSCANINI

Maestri sostituti: Antonio Graziosi - Gino Nastrucci - Giuseppe Papi - Francesco Romei - Maestro istruttore dei cori: Antonio Biondi - Suggeritore: Mario Marchesi - Coreografo e Direttore di scena: Armando Beruccini - FORNITORI: Proprietà delle opere, Ditta G. Ricordi e C. - Scenografo, Mario Sala - Sartoria, Adelchi Zamperoni - Attrezzi, Ditta E. Rancati e C. - Calzoleria, Giosuè Cazzola - Parrucchieri, Biffi e Rampinelli - Elettricista, Alessandro Bezzi e figli - Macchinista, Luigi Bennetti.

La prima recita avrà luogo - salvo casi imprevisti - la sera del giorno 20 Settembre, alle ore 21, coll'opera LA TRAVIATA.

GLOBAL CHARISMA

"I walk and shall always walk
on the straight path that I have traced
for myself in life."

PASSION AND INTRANSIGENCE

The Legend of Toscanini

Prestige, intransigence, an authoritative attitude, and absolute self-referentiality were the characteristics that rapidly came to form an image of Toscanini that later became the norm. A difficult personality, to the extent that he was impossible to deal with when it was a question of imposing his own overall interpretation of a piece of music or even the execution of a single note, or when his stance, his point of view, or his authority were at stake even when it merely concerned the organization of his work. Regarding the conductor's activity in America, Joseph Horowitz wrote: "Toscanini had tolerated no rivals. At the Metropolitan Opera, the New York Philharmonic, and NBC, Gustav Mahler, Willem Mengelberg, Wilhelm Furtwängler, and Leopold Stokowski had challenged his authority and lost."

If conductors of the rank and prestige of the ones mentioned above, as well as the composers with whom he was in contact, could not compete with him victoriously, then neither could the individual performers and even less so the theater managers. Numerous arguments and irreconcilable differences marked Toscanini's very long career and fueled the countless anecdotes about him.

But even more numerous are the expressions of esteem and admiration that at times verged on deference, that he receives from individuals who saw in the maestro not just his outstanding qualities as a musician, but also his moral stature. A quality that was always inextricably linked to the music, and the safeguarding of which could justify the scenes he soon became famous for on both sides of the

Atlantic. The scene recalled by Samuel Antek, violinist for the NBC Symphony Orchestra in all seventeen of the seasons directed by Toscanini, speaks volumes about what it was like to work with him. The orchestra was rehearsing the third movement of Beethoven's much-loved *Ninth*:

We were all very intent. Toscanini was driving on, covered with perspiration, when suddenly he stopped everything. "The celli!" he screamed. "The celli! Not dah-de-dah-h-h, but duy-de dah!" Were they stupid? So-o-o-o, they were taking it easy. They were sitting back in their chairs. There was no bite, no life in the sound! They were insulting Beethoven! They were insulting him! No! Not with Toscanini would they play that horrible way! ... The raging tempest was unleashed. With a torrent of insults he broke his baton, picked up the score, began to pound it, tore it up, kicked at the stand, and pushed it off the stage. Then, bellowing at the top of his lungs, he began to claw at his collar until his hand caught in the chain of the watch he carried in the breast pocket. With a furious wrench he pulled it away, glared at it with unseeing eyes, and, in a vicious lunge, smashed it to the ground where it spilled in all directions. No-o-o! No-o-o! He was through! Finished! He would never conduct this orchestra of jackasses again! He stomped off and walked around the outer rim of the stage, shouting his disgust and smashing his clenched fist violently down on the seats as he passed. We could still hear him after he had left the hall, his oaths reverberating down the corridor as he headed toward his dressing room.

The story goes that the next day Toscanini showed up for the rehearsal as if nothing had happened, but wearing a cheap watch "for rehearsals only."

Anecdotes such as these were what made the most impression on people, ever since the maestro had been invited to La Scala for the first time in 1898. It was from that moment onwards that he began to revolutionize the traditions of Italian musical theater from every artistic and organizational standpoint: for example, by showing the same interest in the stage design and the direction of the performances as he did for the music; by challenging the excessive liberties that the musicians tended to assume, and forbidding the execution of encores; by demanding regular rehearsals for both the singers and the orchestra; by being extremely selective and firing anyone who did not meet his expectations; by establishing a system that required iron discipline from everyone, including the public; and so on. Because of this, his arrival had the effect of a revolution with solid ethical and practical foundations, which did not allow for compromise.

His own conscientiousness was a reflection of that intransigence. An example of this can be found in the description published by the critic Max Smith in the magazine *The Century*, concerning the method Toscanini routinely used to study the score and then proceeded to prepare its execution. According to Smith, the maestro's study of the work, followed by its actual execution, was divided into several distinct and subsequent phases. First, Toscanini played the score on the piano, then, once he had memorized it, he studied it more analytically, almost without a need for the instrument. From that moment onwards, and for all the following phases leading up to and including the performance itself, he would no longer require the score, as it was by then fixed in his mind.

Then he would move on to deal with the singers, whom he prepared individually before putting them together in a group rehearsal. At that point, at a distance from the piano that was being played by the assistant conductor, he clapped his hands to set the rhythm, and at times he himself would sing the parts in unison with the singers, giving directions, orders, criticizing, encouraging, and so on. The next phase was the dress rehearsal accompanied on the piano: during this phase he was greatly involved in emphasizing the opera's dramatic values, teaching the singers the gestures, movements, and expressions, the same way any director would. Lastly, it was time for the orchestra rehearsal and for the rehearsal with everyone involved in the performance on the stage. This part of the process normally went rather smoothly with very few interruptions by virtue of the meticulous work Toscanini had carried out beforehand.

Smith met Toscanini, and then wrote the article for *The Century* on the occasion of the US premiere of Mussorgsky's *Boris Godunov* in New York in 1913. Toscanini had arrived in the city a few years earlier, in 1908, to take over the post of principal conductor of the Metropolitan Opera Company. He had been invited by the impresario of the theater, the Italian Giulio Gatti-Casazza, the man who, a decade earlier, as CEO of La Scala, had hired Toscanini as the theater's artistic director. A successful collaboration was thus reinstated, albeit not without conflict and suspicion between the two men. Their work together lasted until 1915, when Toscanini stepped down from his role for both artistic and personal reasons, probably having to do with the fate of the American soprano Geraldine Farrar, one of the stars of the Metropolitan. Toscanini's affair with Farrar was one of the many he was

alleged to have had. Gatti-Casazza, on the other hand, having in the meantime become the general director of the Metropolitan, remained there until 1935, when he moved back to Italy permanently.

Until his debut at the Metropolitan with Verdi's *Aida*, on November 16, 1908, it was plain to see the caliber of this new conductor. *New York Tribune* critic Henry E. Krehbiel wrote these words:

Of the new conductor it must be said that he is a boon to Italian opera as great as anything that has come out of Italy since Verdi laid down his pen. In the best sense he is an artist, an interpreter, a re-creator. [...] Signor Toscanini brought to the understanding and the emotions of the audience all of Verdi's score, body and soul, as it lives in him, mixing with it an abundance of sympathetic affection.

From 1908 onwards, Toscanini's career developed in a parallel manner between Europe and the United States, with very few interruptions—which coincided with the war—and continuous exchanges, made possible by the tours he went on with La Scala ensemble or the New York Philharmonic Orchestra from one side of the Atlantic to the other. By following the path of his career starting from his arrival in New York, we can get a picture of how it developed: from 1908 to 1915 principal conductor of the Metropolitan Opera Company in New York; from 1920 to 1929 general director of La Scala; from 1926 to 1936 conductor of the New York Philharmonic Orchestra; from 1937 to 1954 principal conductor of the NBC Symphony Orchestra. It was during that lapse of time that the legend of Toscanini took shape and was firmly established.

When he stands, small and silver-haired, in front of a symphony orchestra, he is a furi-

ous perfectionist who makes men play music as they can play it for no other man. It is a good guess that as many Americans know that Toscanini conducts an orchestra as know that Joe DiMaggio plays centerfield.

Thus wrote *Life* magazine on November 27, 1939, dedicating the cover and a long article to the maestro, with photographs that portrayed him as he calmly went about his everyday life in the company of his granddaughter Sonia.

Several years had passed since the conductor had finished working with the New York Philharmonic Orchestra, putting an end to a collaboration that had lasted eleven years and was noticeable for the number of concerts he conducted in the United States and in Europe: 429 concerts, as well as the 23 of the European tour in 1930.

The farewell concert took place on April 29, 1936 at Carnegie Hall, with a program dedicated to the maestro's favorite composers, Beethoven and Wagner, and the participation of the great violinist Jascha Heifetz, who played Beethoven's *Violin Concerto*.

The report of the evening published the next day in the *New York Times* was summed up in the headline emblazoned across the front page: *Toscanini Admirers Storm Hall For His Farewell Concert Here.* Nowadays, it is almost impossible to imagine so much interest and such displays of enthusiasm for a classical musician, although a similar fervour had already characterized Toscanini's American career: like when, on April 13, 1913 at the Metropolitan, while conducting Beethoven's *Ninth*, he stole the limelight from the recent performances of two such star conductors as Gustav Mahler and Felix Weingartner.

Albeit with similar precedents, for the anon-ymous reporter for the *New York Times*, what happened outside and inside Carnegie Hall for Toscanini's farewell to the New York Philharmonic was almost beyond belief:

The conductor's farewell appearance was an event that had few, if any, parallels in New York's musical history. A dynamic, gray-haired little man ended a connection of eleven years with New York's ranking orchestra, and tickets for his final performance were treasured like invaluable jewels.

Those "invaluable jewels" were sold out the first day the concert was announced, with the price of tickets ranging from 10 to 200 dollars apiece, and box office takings worth $23,750. The scalpers who sold tickets at 50 or even 100 dollars more than the official price made a healthy profit.

On the day of the concert there was standing room only for the 140 people who had started gathering at 7:30 a.m., willing to line up on the sidewalk until evening. Desperate last-minute requests for tickets engulfed the phone lines of the newspapers, agencies, and of course, the Philharmonic Orchestra. But it was all to no avail.

At a certain point the situation seemed to be completely out of control, with the police struggling to contain the crowds that, according to an estimate given by the *New York Times*, numbered 5,000, and that even an hour and a half after all the tickets had sold out refused to give up the idea of ever making it inside, and were simply unwilling to believe that all the standing room had been sold out so quickly. At that point the police on horseback had to intervene to get the hordes of people to move back. And in the end, everyone, even those who had traveled hundreds of miles to attend the concert, had to return home greatly disappointed.

Things were not running too smoothly inside, either. It was all the fault of a photographer who, when the concert ended and the applause was at its loudest, dashed to the front of the conductor's podium and took a picture of Toscanini, almost blinding him with the flash. Outraged, the conductor left the stage, determined never to return again. So it was up to Maurice Van Praag, personnel manager of the orchestra, to get up on the stage and address the public that was clamoring for the maestro: "This is the saddest thing I have had to do in my twenty-odd years with the orchestra," he said. "Mr. Toscanini was almost blinded by that flash. He is too upset to take any bows. He is sorry. He asks me to say that he loves you all." Obviously, this did not go over well with the public, which vented its anger by booing and whistling at the other photographers present, after which the culprit was dragged away by the police. Finally, the lights were turned off and the public had no choice but to reluctantly leave.

It was symbolic of how this new phase in Toscanini's career had changed his life. It was a dimension which he struggled to adapt to, a level of fame that until a few years before would have been inconceivable; all the same, he did not want to give up his more direct popularity entirely, of the kind that stemmed from the artist's close contact with the people around him.

That period of Toscanini's career, from 1937 to 1954, is linked to his activity as conductor of the NBC Symphony Orchestra. Toscanini had such a reputation that it could instill a sense of awe in just about anyone—his new orchestra first and foremost. The first impact was described eloquently by the violinist Samuel Antek:

As he stepped up on the podium, by prearranged signal, we all rose, like puppets suddenly propelled to life by a pent-up tension. We had been warned in advance not to make any vocal demonstration and we stood silent, eagerly and anxiously staring.

He looked around, apparently bewildered by our unexpected action, and gestured a faint greeting with both arms, a mechanical smile lighting his pale face for an instant. Somewhat embarrassed, we sat down again. Then, in a rough hoarse voice he called out, "Brahms!" He looked at us piercingly for the briefest moment, then raised his arms. In one smashing stroke, the baton came down. A vibrant sound suddenly gushed forth from the tense players like blood from an artery.

After that Toscanini's baton would come down for some seventeen consecutive NBC radiophonic seasons, from late 1937 to the spring of 1954; and he would leave New York to go on two tours, the last of which when the conductor had reached the ripe old age of 83. The first tour was in 1940 in South America, with 15 concerts in Brazil, Argentina, and Uruguay. The second one was in 1950; called the *Transcontinental United States Tour* it consisted of twenty-one concerts in nineteen cities in sixteen states.

On page 90, Toscanini conducting the NBC Orchestra in one of the many portraits made of the maestro by Robert Hupka, RCA (Radio Corporation of America) sound technician.

Portrait of Toscanini from the program for the concerts held in Paris in November 1934 as director of the "Orchestre des concerts Walther Straram."

Above, group photograph after the premiere of the opera Fra Gherardo *at La Scala in 1928. The conductor and composer of the opera can clearly be identified.*

On the opposite page: several phrases—proof of Toscanini's abruptness toward the performers—annotated on the score by the master prompter Giovanni Semprini during rehearsals for Fra Gherardo.

To the left, Toscanini is infuriated by one of the horns: "Are you a horn? You are the national debt! You have ruined this poor ear of mine! Dunce! You should have been a priest, not a musician!" To the right, he instead reprimands the violas: "Good! Good! Good! Good! This is the way dunces always play! (they repeat) No! No! Slightly better, but still dunces, still shooting yourselves in the foot! (they repeat) No! No! You are ignorant; if you were to be tested you'd all be out on the street! No, no! What terrible thoughts! (one of the musicians mistakes a bow stroke) No, no, don't play like that, don't play like louts, showing no respect for me! When musicians play the way you do, they must expect to be insulted! Your way of playing is a continuous insult to me!"

METICULOUS AND TIRELESS
*Toscanini during concert rehearsals in the last decade of his career: with the great
violinist Jascha Heifetz (1946), with the violinist and conductor Milton Katims (1947),
with the members of the NBC orchestra in Austin, Texas (1950).*

Toscanini in a picture taken in the 1920s.
On the following pages, the New York Philharmonic Symphony Orchestra in 1930 while touring in Europe;
the La Scala ensemble, called "Orchestra Toscanini," at the Milan Conservatory before going on tour around
the United States and Canada, 1920-1921, and the Maestro with the Philharmonic-Symphony Orchestra on its way
to Europe, 1930.

La "Philarmonic Symphony Orchestra„

Primi violini: S. Guidi, « Concertmaster »; H. Lange, « Asst. Conductor »; A. Lichstein; M. Muscanto; R. Henkle; F. Tak; L. A. D'Amico; A. Ribarsch; D. Rosensweig; I. Strassner; A. Belfer; G. Rabinowitz; F. L. Smith; M. de Stefano; J. Gewirtz; A. De Bruille; A. Busch; J. Fishberg.

Secondi violini: I. Pogany, A. Koszegi, F. Lowack, A. Dubensky, R. Heinz, A. Schuller, M. Dayan, S. Tomasso, A. Cores, A. Lora, A. Neveux, M. Freiselman, R. Schenk, L. Sherman, M. Borodkin, S. Levine, A. Stirn, W. Sargaent.

Viole: R. Pollain, M. Cozes, Z. Kurthy, T. Fishberg,

J. J. Kovarik, M. Tartas, M. Gray, M. Barr, S. Lipschitz, L. Verona, G. Imperato, G. Harnisch, B. Bardos, H. Levy.

Violoncelli: A. Wallenstein, J. Emont, O. Giskin, A. Guidi, W. Feder, A. Bass, H. Van Praag, V. Lubalin, R. Stehl, O. Van Koppenhagen, M. Ormandy, M. Caiati.

Contrabassi: A. Fortier, H. Reinshagen, D. Rybb, E. Zickler, M. Tivin, M. Decruck, H. Jenkel, S. Levman, V. Geoffrion, J. De Angelis.

Flauti: J. Amans, A. Ghignatti, J. Fabrizio, B. Gaskins.

Piccol
Oboi:
Corno
Clarin
J. C
Clarin
Clarin
Fagot
Contr
Corni
R.
Trom
Sch

i New York diretta da Toscanini

B. Gaskins.

Labato, G. Apchain, M. Nazzi, A. March.
ese : M. Nazzi.

S. Bellison, O. Conrad, E. Roelofsma,
ardt.

basso : E. Roelofsma.
in mi bem. : J. Gehrhardt.
Kohon, S. Kovar, R. Sensale, W. Conrad.
otto : W. Conrad.
Jaenicke, S. Richart, A. Schulze, L. Ricci,
lze, M. Van Praag.
H. Glantz, N. Prager, L. Konevsky, M.
erg.

Tromboni : M. Falcone, A. Clarke, G. Lucas, R.
Haines.
Tuba : V. Vanni.
Tromba bassa : M. Falcone.
Flicorno : J. J. Perfetto.
Timpani : S. Goodman.
Percussione : A. Schmehl, A. Rich, S. Borodkin,
R. Katz, E. Greinert.
Arpe : T. Cella, Miss. S. Goldner.
Celeste : A. Schuller.
Piano : Z. Kurthy.
Organo : Z. Kurthy.

R.E. CONSERVATORIO - MILANO

ORCHESTRA TOSCANINI

TRAVELING ORCHESTRAS
The tour with the NBC Symphony Orchestra in 1950: on the opposite page, with his son Walter; above, Toscanini (accompanied by his grandson Walfredo) is about to go on tour with the NBC orchestra, and Wilfrid Pelletier with the Metropolitan Opera Association, both of them leaving from New York.

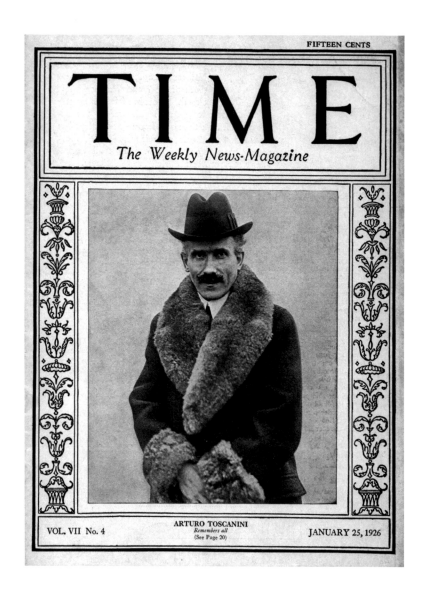

FIFTEEN CENTS

TIME
The Weekly News-Magazine

VOL. VII No. 4

ARTURO TOSCANINI
Remembers all
(See Page 20)

JANUARY 25, 1926

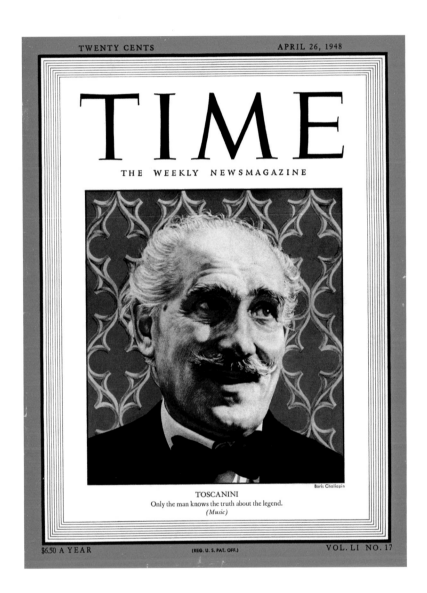

ON THE COVER

Toscanini's media fame can be gauged from the interest shown by the international press, which from the 1920s was endlessly dedicated to the artist's public image and to his private family life.

On the previous pages, feature article in Time, 1948: photographic sequence during the performance of Beethoven with the NBC Symphony Orchestra. On the opposite page, Toscanini on the covers of some of the most important magazines of the day.

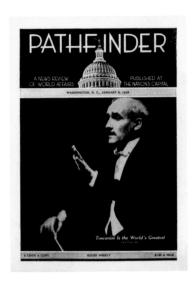

TOSCANINI WATCHING A F
Also Fry Small.

Sid Desfors

Feature article in Time, 1948: Toscanini watching a boxing match on TV.

TOSCANINI'S PRIVATE SIDE
On the cover and on the pages of the November 1939 issue of Life,
Toscanini is portrayed in the company of his granddaughter Sonia,
the daughter of Vladimir Horowitz and Wanda Toscanini.

LIFE

TOSCANINI & GRANDDAUGHTER

NOVEMBER 27, 1939   **10** CENTS

REG. U. S. PAT. OFF.

DER SPIEGEL

DAS DE - MAGAZIN

9. MAI 1951 + 1 DM
ERSCHEINT JEDEN MITTWOCH

V. JAHRGANG
NR.
19

GRANDPA CASANOVA
Nur ein Musiker: Dirigent Toscanini (siehe „Musik")

GUEST OF HONOR
Reception in honor of Toscanini and the general director of the Metropolitan Opera Giulio Gatti-Casazza held at the Hotel St. Regis, New York, on November 22, 1908.

A HISTORICAL CONCERT
*Toscanini's fans standing in line in front of Carnegie Hall
hoping to buy a ticket for the maestro's farewell concert,
performed on April 30, 1936, upon leaving his post as
conductor of the New York Philharmonic Orchestra.*

A CARTOON HERO, TOO
Details from the cartoon by Dino Attanasio for the magazine Tintin, published in Belgium and France, telling the story of Toscanini's life, a few months after the maestro's death in 1957.

AGAINST THE TYRANNY OF FASCISM

Toscanini: Champion of Democracy

Because of my music I have lost three countries, Italy, Germany, and Russia—everywhere people wanted to hear me give political statements and express my beliefs and opinions concerning one party or another—but I am no more than a musician, I want to be free to think, speak, and write what I feel profoundly, and to create my music [...]
A.T. (1937)

I am an old artist who has been among the first to denounce Fascism to the world. I feel and believe that I can act as interpreter of the soul of the Italian people—those people whose voice has been choked for more than twenty years, but, thanks to God, just now is shouting for peace and liberty in the streets and squares of Italy, defying everything, even martial law.
A.T. (1943)

Toscanini's relationship with television was almost exclusively limited to the ten shows produced by NBC between 1948 and 1952. He could have played a more important role if he had accepted the rather lucrative proposals that were made to him by Hollywood.

But in actual fact, he only accepted one of them, which, for once, had little to do with music. This proposal did not come from a Hollywood studio, but from the OWI, the US Office of War Information, an institution set up by President Roosevelt to coordinate war propaganda. The overseas branch of the Office came up with the idea of making a film that would focus on Italy's anti-Fascist core and that would salute its entrance among the ranks of those who fought against Nazism and what had remained of fascism after Mussolini was ousted from power on July 25,

1943. Toscanini was chosen for the film both for his role as orchestra conductor, and as an anti-Fascist exile who had been living and working in the United States for many years.

The phases that had marked his "anti-Fascist" crusade, as it was referred to at the time, were well-known: his decision to no longer conduct in Italy for as long as Mussolini ruled, after being attacked and physically injured in Bologna for having refused to perform the Fascist anthem before a concert; his cable to Hitler protesting against the racial persecutions; his refusal to ever conduct at the Bayreuth Festival again because of the Wagner family's support of the Nazis, and at the Salzburg Festival after Austria's annexation to the Third Reich; his participation in the Lucerne Festival in Switzerland along with other anti-Nazi musicians; his support of the new Palestine Symphony Orchestra formed by Jewish refugees from Central Europe who were denied the right to play; his membership in the Mazzini Society, founded in the United States by Italian exiles. Lastly, on September 13 1943, he signed an open letter "To the People of America" published in *Life* magazine. In the letter—which he wrote together with two other illustrious Italian exiles, the historians Gaetano Salvemini and Giorgio La Piana, and was originally intended as a letter to President Roosevelt—he claimed the right of the Italian people, who had never been the enemies of the Americans, and who had been the first to endure the oppression of a "tyrannical gang of criminals," not to have to pay for the crimes of the Fascist regime.

Because of the many public stances taken by a man who was known for his moral rigor and was famous the world over, Toscanini was the ideal subject for the OWI documentary.

Many years later, Toscanini's son Walter would recall the first time his father was contacted about the project:

The Office of War Information had asked my father to make a propaganda film based on the music from Symphony No. 7 by Shostakovich, which is also known as the symphony that was inspired by the siege and resistance of Leningrad. This proposal was rejected. They came back with another one based on the music of Mozart and Wagner. This too was rejected, and before they could come up with something else I suggested making a film with the music of Verdi and the overture from the Forza del destino, *or that of the* Vespri siciliani, *and the* Hymn of the Nations, *which contains a message of peace and brotherhood.*

To make the film, a group of high-profile collaborators were chosen: Irving Lerner, who would also collaborate with Kubrick and Scorsese many years later, was chosen to produce it; May Sarton was hired for the script; Peter Glushanok and Boris Kaufman for the photography and filming; Alexander Hackenschmied, known as Hammid, as director. The film was made between late 1943 and the start of the following year. The original title was *Toscanini: Hymn of the Nations,* although it was to circulate under other titles as well.

The film was divided into three sections: two musical ones, and a documentary section in the middle. The film begins with Toscanini conducting the overture from the *Forza del destino* performed by the NBC Symphony, and then the scene shifts to his home in Riverdale, where the maestro invites his grandson Walfredo to listen to a recording of the orchestral version of the *Inno di Garibaldi,* a famous song from the Italian Risorgimento. The scene is accompanied by voiceover as follows:

Every week, the magic of radio brings the music of Arturo Toscanini to millions of Americans. America has taken Toscanini to its heart, not only as a musician of unmatchable talent, but also as a champion of democracy. In his house above the Hudson River in New York, he has found a haven of freedom for his children and grandchildren. But his thoughts have never been far from his beloved Italy.

Americans know that this son of a soldier of Garibaldi refused to allow his music to become the servant of tyrants. They know that twenty years ago he took his stand against the tyranny of fascism in his own land. When the Fascists rose to power in Germany, Toscanini withdrew from Bayreuth. When Austria was forced into the Reich, Toscanini was heard no more at Salzburg. And when the night of fascism darkened most of Continental Europe, he brought his music and his democratic faith to the New World. He was not alone. Other Italians who preferred exile to slavery were carrying on the fight in America.

After showing the images of other illustrious Italian exiles in the United States, from the historian Gaetano Salvemini to the politician Luigi Sturzo, the scene shifts to the studios of the radio station, and to the moment when Mussolini falls from power on July 25. "This is the day for which millions of Americans of Italian descent have been waiting," says the voice from off-stage. The scene then goes back to Toscanini's home, where the maestro, seated at the piano, is practicing Verdi's *Hymn of the Nations*. It is the prologue to the last part of the movie. The scene is again accompanied by the off-stage commentary: "This was the day. Arturo Toscanini had his answer ready. And his answer was music." And finally, "Arturo Toscanini had last conducted it in Italy in 1915, during another war forced on civilization by the German military regime. Now from New York, the music went out to celebrate Italy's new renaissance and freedom."

The third part of the film entirely consists of the *Hymn of the Nations* that Toscanini directed during that month of December at NBC's Studio 8-H, with the station's orchestra, the Westminster College Choir, and the tenor Jan Peerce as soloist.

The *Hymn* is a composition of circumstance intended for the 1862 International Exhibition in London, which Verdi had accepted to compose, although against his will. The composition was not accepted by the Exhibition's Musical Board, whose reasons were hardly convincing. All the same, it was performed to great acclaim at Her Majesty's Theatre in Haymarket, London. What was particular about the composition, which is no doubt why it was chosen for the movie, is that in the final part Verdi had chosen the music from three "national anthems," for the purpose of musically relating Italy, a country that had just been founded, to the two countries that were politically closest to it: England and France. That is why Verdi had chosen the royal anthem *God Save the Queen*, the *Marseillaise* for France, and, for Italy, the music the composer Michele Novaro had written in 1848 for *Il canto degli Italiani*, more commonly referred to as *Fratelli d'Italia* (not with the original words by Goffredo Mameli, but with those written especially by Arrigo Boito for the *Hymn of the Nations*).

This is not the place to discuss the details of the choices made by Verdi in that situation, for neither *The Marseillaise* nor *Il canto degli Italiani* were as yet the official anthems of France and Italy (they would become so in 1876 and 1946, respectively). However, in Toscanini's eyes and in those of the people involved in the movie the fact that a famous composer like Verdi had written music uniting some of the nations that in late 1943 found themselves in a common front against Nazi Germany must have seemed like an excellent opportunity. Only two countries were missing: the United States and the Soviet Union. However, as Walter Toscanini again recalled later, the solution was easy: "While the movie was being made they came to me to ask whether, besides the American anthem, the Russian one, which at the time was still *The Internationale*, could also be added at the very end." Toscanini was pleased with the idea, and at the end of the piece by Verdi, he added the Russian anthem first, followed by *The Star-Spangled Banner* as a conclusion. Unfortunately, the film had already been produced when the news came out that the Soviet Union had abandoned the *Internationale*—the old anthem of the Paris Commune which in 1918 had been chosen by the new State that had emerged from the revolution the year before—and had adopted a new one, which is still the anthem today. Walter Toscanini recalled that:

But at that point the strangest and most unexpected thing occurred: when everything had already been played, sung, recorded, filmed, and the crew was working on the editing, Russia decided to demote [...] the Internationale; *it was no longer the national anthem, and a brand new one was adopted in its place!*
So the people from the Office of War Information, who were very alarmed, told us to remove the Internationale *and replace it with the newly adopted anthem.*
Naturally, my father absolutely refused to be a party to this political opportunism and said that if the Internationale *was cut from the film, it being the anthem of the lower classes and of all the workers of the world, then the film should simply not be released at all.*

And that is indeed what happened. Except for the fact that in the version of the movie that was distributed the *Internationale* had judiciously been cut. The film was finally released in its original edition in 1988, first by Blackhawk and then by United Films, sponsored by the Library of Congress.

Toscanini had always been rather intolerant of the hypocrisy and conventionalisms of politics, whatever their source may have been. To the extent that, after the war, and after returning to Italy, when the Italian Parliament appointed him a Senator for life, he refused to accept. He declared that although he was very honored, he had always been against acknowledgments, academic titles, and decorations of any kind, and so he wished to live the rest of his life with the same simplicity as always.
For Toscanini, his political action was direct, that of a "democracy militant" as he was called by a newspaper, expressed via acts of great symbolic value, such as his public rejection of Nazism, or by direct actions of moral or practical support, such as his conducting of a military band just a stone's throw away from the front during the First World War, or of concerts to collect funds in favor of the victims of war or for other noble charitable aims. His Red Cross Benefit Concert held on May 25, 1944 at Madison Square Garden, which was jam-packed, brought in "the largest amount ever realized from the sale of tickets for any performance of serious music," according to the *New York Times*. On that occasion, his baton was auctioned off at $11,000 by New York Mayor Fiorello La Guardia.
Mayor La Guardia also went to visit him in Milan in the summer of 1946, after the maestro's arrival in Italy a few months before. It had been his triumphal return for the solemn reopening of La Scala after it was rebuilt due to the damage caused by the Allied bombing in 1943. Toscanini himself had contributed to the expenses. In previous years, there had

been signs that he might be coming back to Italy, when anonymous posters and words appeared on the theater walls praising him.

But the time was not right yet, seeing that in May 1945, with a message broadcast by the *Voice of America*, he declined La Scala ensemble's invitation to conduct it once again: although he was profoundly moved by the gesture, he would never go back so long as there was a monarchy, explicitly accused of "being an accomplice to the crimes committed by the Fascists in its name." "I will be happy to return amongst you as the citizen of a free Italy, and not as a subject of the king and the princes of the House of Savoy," was how he ended his message. These were harsh words, that undeniably triggered the bitter protests of the monarchists. Not to mention the many who over the years accused him of having been an accomplice to the air raids on Italy's cities.

But in the end, Toscanini did return, and he did so even before the popular referendum that was held to decide whether Italy was to become a Republic, or remain a monarchy. And his message was heard by the listeners of the *Voice of America*, although the parts that related to the Savoys were cut. Political convenience had had the upper hand, and the following year Toscanini wanted to express, through his daughter Wally, the hope that "finally those around him would only speak of him as an artist; that, by putting aside the politics that had taken him away from his country, his country would be willing to welcome back only a messenger of art, and that it only desired to see and wait for him with that identity."

"Italy is free. Toscanini may return," were the words written on the pamphlet that appeared in Milan in April 1946. On May 11 his wishes finally came true. *Corriere della Sera*

critic Franco Abbiati crowned the event with great, understandable emphasis: "Toscanini came by La Scala last night like the wise old man of the fables who returns to his love who once wept for him, but now finds him safe and strong in faith and in his teachings."

Afterwards, Toscanini went back to conducting in Europe, and at La Scala in particular, almost each year, although he mainly worked for the NBC Symphony Orchestra for the rest of his days. He spent his last years between Villa Pauline in Riverdale and his homes in Italy, in Milan and on the Isolino on Lake Maggiore. Politics no longer interfered much with his desire to finally be considered a "messenger of art" and nothing more than that, as he had always demanded and hoped for.

On page 130, Toscanini arriving in Haifa to conduct the Palestine Symphony Orchestra, founded by the famous violinist Bronislaw Huberman and made up of Jewish musicians from Central Europe.

THE CLASH WITH MUSSOLINI

Above, Toscanini and Mussolini at La Scala in the early 1920s. To the right of the conductor, the soprano Toti Dal Monte.

On the opposite page, a typewritten copy of the letter written by Toscanini to Mussolini informing him that he was physically attacked in Bologna on May 14, 1931. On the occasion of a commemorative concert for the composer Giuseppe Martucci, the maestro was attacked for refusing to play the Fascist party anthem before the performance. Afterwards, Toscanini resolved never to perform in Italy for as long as Mussolini was in power.

A sua Ecc. BENITO MUSSOLINI

Ieri sera mentre mi recavo colla mia famiglia al Teatro Communale
di Bologna per compiervi un gentile atto d'amore e d'amicizia alla
memoria di Giuseppe Martucci - invitatovi del Podestà della sudetta
Città non per una serata di gala, ma per una artistica commemorazione -
venni aggredito e colpito replicatamente al viso da una masnada
inqualificabile, presente in Bologna il Sottosegretario agli Interni.
Non soddisfatta di ciò la masnada, ingrossatasi nelle sue fila, si
recava sotto le finestre dell Hotel Brun, dove abitavo - emettendo
ogni sorta di contumelie e minaccie al mio indirizzo - non solo -
ma uno di suoi capi, per il tramite del Maestro Respighi, m'ingiungeva
di lasciare Bologna entro le sei antimeridiane, non garentendo, caso
contrario, la mia incolumità.
Questo communico a V.E. perchè sia per il silenzio della stampa
o per fallaci ed inesatte informazioni V.E. non potesse avere
esatte notizie del fatto, e perche del fatto rimanga memoria. Ossequi

                                        Arturo Toscanini

IN PALESTINE

Toscanini on the Dead Sea during a trip to Palestine in 1938. From 1936 onward Toscanini traveled there twice to direct and support the Palestine Symphony Orchestra. On one of those occasions, on January 24, 1937, he wrote to a friend of his "If only you knew how much good my presence did in Palestine! Modesty doesn't allow me to elaborate, but I can assure you that I won and was enriched by much love. I am loved by many more people today."

Award in recognition of Toscanini's opposition to the malevolent treatment of Jewish artists in Germany.

*With Bronislaw Huberman at the end
of a concert where he conducted
the Palestine Symphony Orchestra.*

LUCERNE: A FESTIVAL IN THE NAME OF FREEDOM

*Poster and photo of the concert conducted by Toscanini in Lucerne,
Switzerland, on August 29, 1939, with the participation of the famous Russian
pianist Vladimir Horowitz, who had married the maestro's daughter Wanda
in 1933. Toscanini's relationship with Lucerne had begun in 1938 after his
decision to cease participating in the Salzburg Festival when Austria was
annexed to Nazi Germany.*

EINSTEIN'S PRAISE

Letter written by Albert Einstein, sent from Princeton on March 1, 1936, in which the scientist praises Toscanini for his firm stance against fascism and support for the Jewish cause. Einstein's letter is just one of the letters of praise received by Toscanini during that period from all over the world. This is what Einstein wrote: "Dear Maestro! I feel it is my duty to tell you how much I admire and revere you. You are not just an unparalleled interpreter of universal musical literature, whose forms deserve our utmost admiration. You have also proven that you are a man of great dignity in the fight against the fascist criminals. I am also profoundly grateful to you for having given such great meaning to the new orchestra that is being formed in Palestine. The fact that a contemporary like you exists dispels many of the disappointments that one is continually subjected to by the minorum gentium species! Fondly and respectfully, yours, A. Einstein."

Princeton 1. III. 36.

Herrn Toscanini, New York.

Verehrter Meister!

Es ist mir Bedürfnis, Ihnen
einmal zu sagen, wie sehr ich
Sie bewundere und verehre.
Sie sind nicht nur der unerreichbare
Interpret der musikalischen Welt-
Literatur, dessen Gestaltungen
die höchste Bewunderung verdient.
Sie haben auch im Kampfe gegen
die fascistischen Verbrecher sich
als ein Mann von höchster Würde
gezeigt. Auch empfinde ich tiefste
Dankbarkeit dafür, dass Sie dem
neu zu gründenden Palästina-Orchester
eine Förderung von unschätzbarer
Bedeutung in Aussicht gestellt
haben.

Die Thatsache, dass es einen solchen
Zeitgenossen gibt, wiegt viele Ent-
täuschungen auf, welche man
an der species minorum gentium
ohne Ende erleben muss!

In Liebe und hoher Verehrung
grüsst Sie herzlich Ihr
A. Einstein.

TOSCANINI THE "REFUGEE"
Toscanini and his wife Carla apply for a permit to travel in the United States during the Second World War. Toscanini is headed to Washington to conduct the Philadelphia Orchestra.

A STAR AND MORE THAN THAT

Toscanini and the Media

On the occasion of his last concert with the New York Philharmonic Orchestra, which had ended with his stubborn refusal to return to the stage because of the brazenness of a photographer, Toscanini had asked that the box office earnings be divided between all those who had worked with him in those years: orchestra members, doormen, ushers, the whole staff of Carnegie Hall, including stenographers and telephone operators, and all those who worked in the offices of the Philharmonic Orchestra. He even donated some of the money to the orchestra's pension fund. It was yet another occasion for Toscanini to directly reveal the temperament he was famous for, and that was much harder to get a real feel for when it was merely described on radio shows or in the newspapers.

However, we cannot overlook the fact that it was because of the radio and the newspapers that an orchestra conductor could be as popular as a star athlete like Joe DiMaggio. The audience Toscanini could hope for in Europe was nothing compared not just with the thousands of people who rushed to attend his last concert with the Philharmonic Orchestra, but above all with the many more who had listened to the concert on the radio. The proof lies in the fact that, after the concert, many listeners flooded the radio station, the newspapers, and Carnegie Hall with phone calls anxious to know more about Toscanini's health, after hearing him described on the radio by Van Praag as having been "almost blinded."

Based on such precedents it is easy to believe the news according to which the following year, when Toscanini began to collaborate with the NBC Symphony Orchestra, the organizers were overwhelmed with almost 50,000 requests for tickets to his concert, likewise to be aired on the radio, at NBC headquarters.

Toscanini's arrival in the world of broadcasting was the crowning of all the efforts made by David Sarnoff, president of RCA, which NBC was affiliated with, aimed at earning the permanent collaboration of a celebrity capable of appealing to huge numbers of people from all walks of life. From that moment onwards, the albeit famed orchestra conductor began to embody the very symbol of that category also for a public that did not necessarily only include classical music lovers. The earliest means of mass communication, the daily newspapers, magazines, and above all the radio all brought Toscanini's name and music to the homes of millions of American citizens, even to those who would never have dreamed of crowding the sidewalk outside of Carnegie Hall for a place to stand and listen to his concert inside. Toscanini's NBC debut was aired on Christmas Eve, 1937. For Sarnoff's RCA it was a hugely successful media and marketing operation, as the work went beyond the radio and recording businesses, and also included the production of radiophonic systems, gramophones, and records. For the sector, Toscanini undoubtedly represented a valuable resource and a good business prospect. As Max Smith had already written in *Century Magazine* in 1913:

A man like Toscanini is worth more than any one 'star' even in financial terms. That is why the Italian conductor's services are now in demand in every musical center of the world, enabling him to earn in a year almost twice as much as the President of the United States.

At the time, Toscanini's renown did not just stem from his live performances but from many other activities as well. By that time he had been accepting requests to make records for a long time. Between 1920 and 1921 he made his first recordings for the Victor Talking Machine Company in Camden, New Jersey, with the Scala ensemble with which he was touring the United States and Canada during a period when the Milan theater was closed for renovation.

It was an impressive *tour de force* that in over three months brought the orchestra to forty-three cities, with as many as sixty-one concerts. From December to March, moreover, the orchestra stopped in Camden, New Jersey, for its recording sessions. The result of these sessions were fourteen poor-quality records, which Toscanini would criticize and regret having made.

The pieces they played were mostly single movements from symphonies and instrumental numbers from operas, adapted to meet the requirements and the limited capacity of the recording studios and the records of that day and age. The music was by a variety of composers: Bizet, Berlioz, Beethoven, Donizetti, Massenet, Mendelssohn, Mozart, Pizzetti, Wolf-Ferrari and, a choice that might come as a surprise, an ancient Renaissance dance by Vincenzo Galilei, the father of the celebrated scientist Galileo, which had been orchestrated by Ottorino Respighi.

Those 78 rpm records, recorded on one or both sides, which Toscanini had made unwillingly, did not just serve to cover some of the expenses for the tour, but little by little they began to forge a new image of the conductor, whose name was associated for the first time with sounds that could be listened to even by those who had never seen him in person. It was a genuine revolution, whose importance is hard to grasp today. Yet effective proof of the remarkable power of seduction of those early records by Toscanini can be found in the anecdote told by the New York critic and historian Irving Kolodin:

The year was 1923. My school had an orchestra where I was also a member. And the group, besides the teacher who instructed and conducted it, included some older students who were at times given the chance to conduct it. We played around and called the most talented one, who was also my best friend, "Arturo." His name could have been Alexander or John or Meyer, but it definitely wasn't Arturo. We called him Arturo because one or two years before Arturo Toscanini, while on tour in the United States with the Scala ensemble, had made some recordings. We knew very little about that tour, but when the records came out a few months later we realized that those raw sounds (today they're the sounds of an out-of-tune organ filtered by a good amount of wadding) were in themselves models to be imitated. And the models were so convincing that anyone who conducted in a similar manner, no matter how distant from that example, was nicknamed "Arturo."

Walter Toscanini, the maestro's son, described how the first gramophone that entered their home was a gift from Enrico Caruso, and that, although everyone in the family was very excited to see what the new invention was like, only the maestro was unimpressed. The first thing he did was criticize the fact that the tenor's voice was greatly distorted, and that there were all sorts of background noises on the recording itself. His attitude was the same when it came to judging the records made by the German conductor Artur Nikisch, whose amazing talent was not done justice to in the recordings—to the extent that Toscanini found it hard to understand why he had authorized their publication.

Even in episodes such as these Toscanini was true to himself. As always, music came before everything else: it was an ideal that wouldn't allow for compromise, not even when it was a question of something new that, however imperfect it may have been, already clearly showed its potential as a new resource for the diffusion of musical culture.

Toscanini, in fact, never hid his doubts about that technology, which could not guarantee, as he would have wanted, respect for the musical values that he believed were essential. As Peter Hugh Reed wrote in *Record Guide*, he had always believed that music that is reproduced is never, even in the best of cases, equal to the real thing. Instead, in his opinion, it should reproduce the sounds of the instruments and the perfect balance between them, just like in a concert hall.

For Toscanini, in other words, not even the fact that this was a great opportunity to bring music to the homes of millions of people, thanks to a record or to the radio, was enough to make him accept the poor quality of the recordings. On the other hand, it was quite natural that for him, even when he conducted for programs on the radio or to make recordings, the yardstick was the experience he had matured from the early years of the previous century, when radio and the record album didn't even exist or were not as yet part of the usual activity of a musician, or even less so of an orchestra conductor.

Indeed, Toscanini always sought the feelings that were aroused in him while listening to live music, even when it meant listening to music recorded at Villa Pauline, his home in Riverdale, where the RCA technicians had set up a huge audio system that could practically be heard in all the rooms. But the most impressive installation involved the three columns of loudspeakers in the hall, where the maestro generally listened to music, and always at full volume. It was the attitude of a person who could not resign himself to a dimension that would not offer him the same experience that he was accustomed to.

And yet, from the second half of the 1930s, the name Toscanini would forever be associated with the radio and recordings. And even today, his image as a conductor cannot be separated from the huge collection of recordings to which were added, from the winter between 1920 and 1921, along with those of the Scala ensemble, ones with the New York Philharmonic, the BBC Symphony, Philadelphia Orchestra and, lastly, the NBC Symphony Orchestra, which were even more numerous. Together with the NBC Symphony Orchestra he even took part in ten televised shows between 1948 and 1952, the first of which was dedicated to Wagner. It was also one of the first concerts ever to be televised, on March 20, 1948, preceded only an hour or so before by the CBS broadcast of the Philadelphia Orchestra conducted by Eugene Ormandy.
It was the start of the fierce competition which came to dominate the music market, as well as television. But Toscanini would stay out of the fray: he was too old by then, and he had in any case always had little enthusiasm for technological innovations when it came to music.

On page 150, Toscanini views the film Toscanini: Hymn of the Nations, *promoted by the US Office of War Information, which coordinated US war propaganda, and made in New York between late 1943 and the start of the following year.*

On the opposite page, Toscanini using a radio broadcasting device in the mid-1930s, in a photo taken by his son Walter.

Sammlung W. Toscanini

**IN THE HOMES
OF THE AMERICAN PEOPLE**
*Toscanini during a concert taped for
television. The conductor and the NBC
Orchestra made ten recordings to be aired
on television between 1948 and 1952.*

156

ON AIR
Toscanini during a TV show in 1950 and while the film
Toscanini: Hymn of the Nations *was being made in late 1943.*

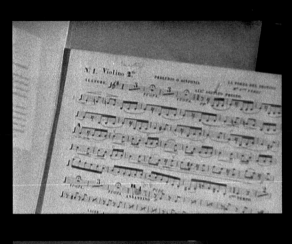

Above, Toscanini in three photographs from the 1930s, pictured with David Sarnoff, President of RCA – Radio Corporation of America, Maurice van Praag, manager of the New York Philharmonic Orchestra, and Samuel Chotzinoff, musical consultant and producer for NBC – National Broadcasting Company.
On the following pages, photographic sequence on the occasion of the last public concert with the NBC Symphony Orchestra, April 4, 1954.

33133 K
33133 K
33133 K
PANCHROMATIC
ILFORD
ILFORD
H P 3
11
11A
12
12A
13
13A
1
1A
2
2A
3
3A

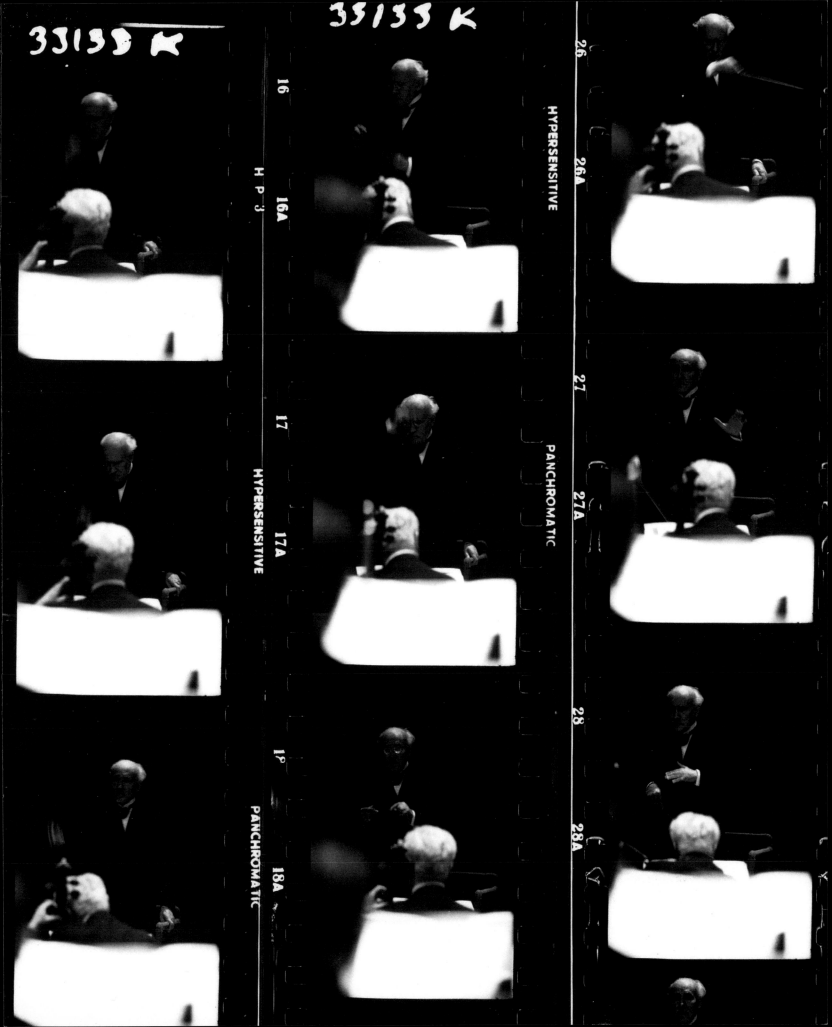

MOMENTS OF A REMARKABLE LIFE

"Everyone welcomes me here,
everyone is in a state of delirium for me!
It's as if they were seeing and hearing me
for the first time!"

FAMILY MEMORIES
Above, Arturo Toscanini at four years of age, 1871.
Opposite page, Arturo and his sister Narcisa with their Aunt Esterina, 1875.

Two pictures dated to the end of the century. Above he is shown with a beard, along with his son Walter, and his brother-in-law Enrico Polo and his son Riccardo.

On these and the following pages,
two images that portray Toscanini
in rather different situations. The first
photo shows Toscanini in 1909,
at a time when there are still no signs
of the bloodbath that would strike
Europe, as he is about to board the
INKA aerostatic balloon anchored
in front of the gas plant in Milan.
The second image is dated to 1917,
during the First World War, and shows
Toscanini conducting a military fanfare
near the front line on the Isonzo River.
During those years he conducted many
charity concerts in favor of the war
victims, and when the conflict ended
he was awarded a Silver Medal
of Military Valor.

"I cried like a baby, and in the general's presence I was as stupid as a goose. And I feel overwhelmed by this great symbol of honor, which I don't think I deserve. What could have been more humble or simple than to take a few wind players and a little music to Monte Santo, in the midst of those dear soldiers who conquered it?"

Toscanini in Salzburg in the early 1930s, in the company of the orchestra conductor Bruno Walter (left) and the writer Thomas Mann.

This image and the ones on the following pages indicate the difficult situation Toscanini found himself in because of his concrete support of the fight against Nazi Fascism: on the one hand, he became the symbol of an absolute ideal of freedom and justice, and was for this reason chosen to star in the war propaganda film Toscanini: Hymn of the Nations; on the other, for the same reason, he was accused by some people of being a party to those who bombed the Italian cities during the war. Moreover, Toscanini's condemnation, pronounced on more than one occasion, of the King of Italy Victor Emmanuel III—whom he referred to as a "degenerate"—and of his dynasty, whom he believed were equally responsible for the evils of fascism, also caused those who favored the Italian monarchy to be hostile to him. This was the atmosphere that surrounded the bitter exchange of letters between Toscanini and Gian Luca Cicogna in 1943, to whom the one reproduced on the following pages is addressed.

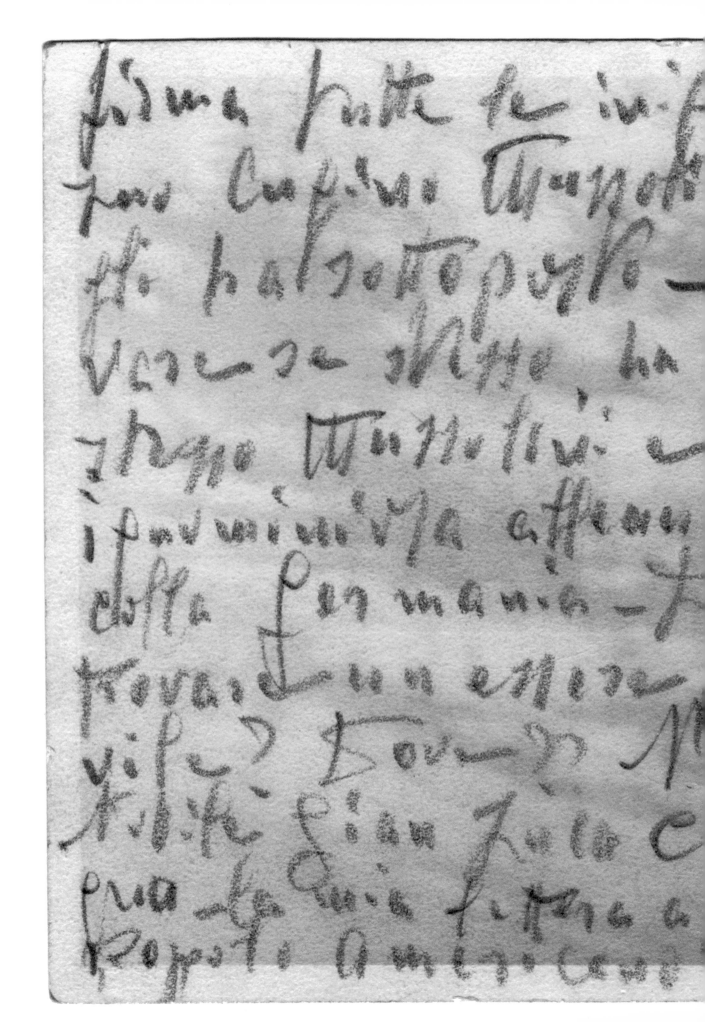

On this and the following pages,
La Scala after the air raids, in 1943,
and the anonymous posters lauding
Toscanini.

185

GLIAMO
SCANINI

"I was very happy to be back in Italy, very happy to have resumed contact with my orchestra and my audience at La Scala. I can't describe the emotion I felt at my first concert! I was afraid of fainting on stage!"

On these and the previous pages, the concert
for the reopening of La Scala held on May 11, 1946.

RETURN TO MILAN

Above, Toscanini in Milan with Mayor of New York Fiorello La Guardia, who visited him in the summer of 1946. The maestro had just returned to Italy a few months earlier. On the opposite page, La Scala rebuilt, 1950.

The final concert at La Scala, with a program dedicated to Wagner,
held on September 19, 1952.

At La Scala, in December 1954. In the audience with conductors Victor De Sabata and Antonino Votto (seen from behind), and Maria Callas at a rehearsal for the opera La vestale *by Gaspare Spontini, the opening performance of the season.*

FORMIDABLE ENCOUNTERS

On this and the following pages, images that bear witness to Toscanini's relationships and encounters with some of the most famous names in music in the past century: Claude Debussy, Ernest Ansermet in Lucerne, Guido Cantelli among the members of the New York Philharmonic orchestra, Victor De Sabata in the audience of La Scala, Ildebrando Pizzetti in the days of Fra Gherardo, Enrico Caruso. Lastly, during a party in the home of the soprano Frances Alda, in the company of some of the greatest performers, such as the tenor Giovanni Martinelli, the baritone Giuseppe De Luca, and the soprano Maria Jeritza.

On these and the following pages, moments in the maestro's private life during the final years, between his villa in Riverdale, New York, and his houses in Milan with soprano Rose Bampton (on page 206), his daughter Wally (on page 210) and on Isolino di San Giovanni in the company of his granddaughter Emanuela di Castelbarco (on page 212).

"I firmly believe that the best part of myself, the one that can clearly shed light on my soul, remains and will always remain unexpressed. Only a few truly superior beings, like Dante, Shakespeare, Leopardi, Beethoven, Verdi, Wagner, are given the chance to wholly express themselves for the joy of humanity."

JANUARY 16, 1957
*Italian newspaper headlines
reporting Toscanini's death,
in Riverdale, New York.*

215

MILAN PAYS TRIBUTE TO TOSCANINI
Toscanini's funeral, February 18, 1957.
On page 220, a bust of Toscanini made by Adolfo Wildt in 1923,
Milan, Ridotto della Scala.

"There have, of course, been other great conductors… but the Maestro was the only one who knew how to get you to play better than you thought you could. This gift is allowed only to the gods, and in this sense he was a god."

EDWIN BACHMANN,
VIOLINIST WITH THE NBC ORCHESTRA

TIMELINE
1867
1957

1876

Enrolls at the Royal School of Music in Parma.
Plays the cello in a number of school recitals
and for five seasons of the Teatro Regio.

1895

On December 22 he makes his
conducting debut as artistic
director of the Teatro Regio
in Turin, where, on February 1,
1896 he will conduct the world
premiere of *La bohème*
by Giacomo Puccini.

1867

Born in Parma on March 25, the
first of the four children of Claudio
Toscanini and Paola Montani.

1885

Earns a diploma in cello and
composition with highest honors.

1886

Engaged as the principal cellist of the Italian opera
company headed by the impresario Claudio Rossi, on tour
at the Teatro Imperial of Rio de Janeiro in Brazil. At the
last moment, he is called upon to replace the ensemble's
regular conductor. The first opera he conducts is Verdi's
Aida. During this period he also conducts several world
premieres, including: *Edmea* by Alfredo Catalani on
November 4, 1886, at the Teatro Carignano in Turin;
Pagliacci by Ruggero Leoncavallo on May 21, 1892, at the
Teatro Dal Verme in Milan.

1900

His daughter Wally is born.

1901

On January 27 Giuseppe Verdi dies. On February 1 Toscanini conducts the commemorative concert at La Scala, and on February 26 he conducts "Va', pensiero" of the moving of the bodies of Verdi and Giuseppina Strepponi from the Cimitero Monumentale to the Casa di Riposo per Musicisti. His son Giorgio is born.

1906-1908

Toscanini's father Claudio and his son Giorgio die.
His daughter Wanda is born.
He leaves the directorship of La Scala and takes over that of the Metropolitan Opera Company in New York.

1897

Marries Carla De Martini on June 21.

1898-1903

His son Walter is born.
Toscanini leaves the Teatro Regio in Turin and upon the advice of Arrigo Boito and Giulio Gatti-Casazza, the theater's administrative director, he takes over the directorship of Milan's Teatro alla Scala. On December 26, 1898, he debuts at La Scala with Wagner's *Die Meistersinger von Nürnberg*.
At La Scala he conducts Verdi's *Il trovatore*, an opera that at the time was considered to have been surpassed, thus laying the foundations for the "Verdi renaissance."

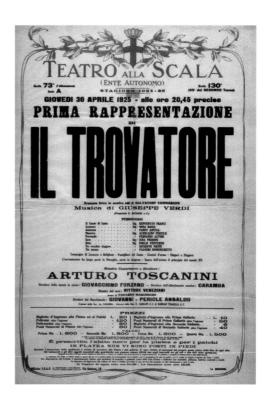

1910

On December 10, in New York, he conducts the world premiere of Giacomo Puccini's *La fanciulla del West*.

1913

In Italy, he takes part in the celebration of the first centennial of Giuseppe Verdi's birth, conducting *La traviata* and *Falstaff* in Busseto, and then the *Messa da Requiem*, and *Falstaff* at La Scala.

1920

Nominated "plenipotentiary director of La Scala," and asked to reform the opera house both from an artistic and an organizational standpoint. Between 1920 and 1921 he tours the United States and Canada with the La Scala ensemble, holding 61 concerts in many cities. During that period he also makes his first records for the Victor Talking Machine Company in Camden, New Jersey.

1915-1917

On July 26 he conducts a concert at the Arena di Milano with an ensemble of musicians before an audience of 40,000, and 150 wounded soldiers. The program is entirely dedicated to Verdi, and ends with patriotic songs. Conducts a military fanfare near the front line on the Isonzo river.

1924

On May 1, in Milan, Toscanini conducts the world premiere of Arrigo Boito's *Nerone*. His mother, Paola Montani, dies.

1926

On April 25, in Milan, he conducts the world premiere of *Turandot* by Puccini, who died in 1924. From 1926 to 1936 his collaboration with the New York Philharmonic Orchestra develops; as its principal conductor he takes the ensemble on a tour of the United States and Europe and produces numerous records.

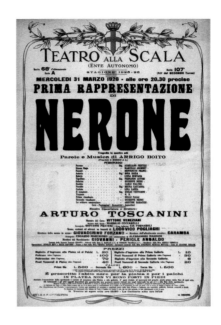

1929

At the end of a successful tour by the La Scala ensemble in Vienna and Berlin, he leaves the artistic directorship of the Milanese theater.

1930

Richard Wagner's son, Siegfried, invites Toscanini—the first non-German-school conductor—to the Festpielhaus in Bayreuth, the Bavarian theater consecrated to the cult of the German composer. Over the course of two seasons, 1930 and 1931, Toscanini conducts *Tristan und Isolde*, *Tannhäuser*, and *Parsifal* in Bayreuth. As a sign of his great esteem for Wagner, the conductor does not accept payment for his work.

1931

On May 14, in Bologna, on the occasion of a commemorative concert for the composer Giuseppe Martucci, Toscanini is attacked and physically injured for refusing to play the Fascist party anthem. After the episode, he decides he will no longer conduct in Italy as long as Mussolini is in power.

1938

Takes part in the Lucerne Festival in Switzerland with other musicians against Nazism who, like Toscanini, decide they will no longer perform at the Salzburg Festival after Austria's annexation to Hitler's Reich.

1939

Joins the Mazzini Society, founded in the United States by Italian exiles. From 1939 to 1945 he principally works in the United States, with the exception of a tour with the NBC Symphony Orchestra in South America (Argentina, Brazil, Uruguay) in 1940.

1933

Together with others, he signs a protest cable addressed to Hitler against racial persecution. During the same year, Hitler invites Toscanini to conduct in Bayreuth once more, but the conductor refuses, owing to Wagner family's sympathies for Nazism. His daughter Wanda and the Russian pianist Vladimir Horowitz are married.

1936

Retires from the New York Philharmonic. Toscanini travels to Israel, where he holds concerts to support the Palestine Symphony Orchestra, founded by the Polish violinist Bronislaw Huberman, comprised of Jewish refugees from Central Europe.

1937

He conducts his last lyric operas performed in a theater at the Salzburg Festival. From then on, he devotes his work to the symphonic repertoire and lyric operas in concert form. On December 25 Toscanini begins his collaboration—made possible by David Sarnoff, President of RCA, Radio Corporation of America—with the NBC, National Broadcasting Company Orchestra, the New York station affiliated with RCA.

1943

Supports the "war bond" and the Red Cross. He plays himself in the propaganda film *Toscanini: Hymn of the Nations* produced by the OWI (US Office of War Information), in which he conducts Verdi's *Hymn of the Nations*, adding the national anthems of the Soviet Union and the United States at the end.

1946

When the war ends he returns to Italy, where, from May 11 to June 24, 1946, he conducts four concerts at La Scala for the reopening of the theater, rebuilt after the damage caused by the Allied bombs.

1954

On April 4 he conducts his last public concert with the NBC Symphony Orchestra. It is an all Wagner program.

1948

On March 20, in New York, at NBC headquarters, he conducts one of the first concerts filmed by a TV station. It is an all Wagner program.

1950

He goes on the Transcontinental United States Tour with the NBC Symphony Orchestra, traveling to 20 cities and 16 different states.

1951

Carla, his wife, dies.

1952

In September he conducts his last concert at La Scala. It is an all Wagner program.

1957

Dies at his home in Riverdale, New York, on January 16. On February 18 he is buried in the Cimitero Monumentale in Milan.

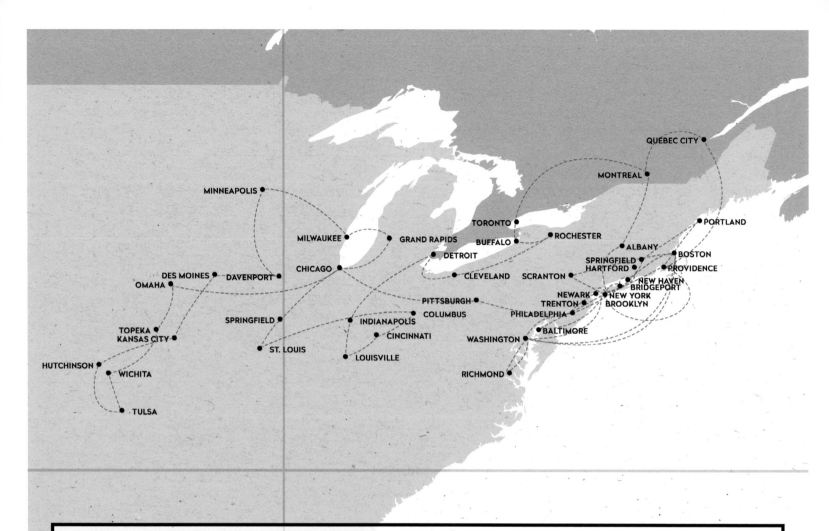

ORCHESTRA DELLA SCALA, TOUR IN US AND CANADA, 1920-1921

1920
28 December .... **NEW YORK**, Metropolitan Opera House
29 December .... **BALTIMORE**
30 December .... **PHILADELPHIA**, Academy of Music

1921
1 January .... **BROOKLYN**, Academy of Music
3 January .... **NEW YORK**, Carnegie Hall
4 January .... **SPRINGFIELD** (Massachusetts)
5 January .... **PORTLAND** (Maine)
7 January .... **BOSTON**, Symphony Hall
8 January .... **SAME VENUE**
9 January .... **PROVIDENCE**
11 January .... **NEW YORK**, Metropolitan Opera House
12 January .... **NEWARK**
15 January .... **PHILADELPHIA**, Academy of Music
16 January .... **NEW YORK**, Hippodrome
17 January .... **WASHINGTON D.C.**
18 January .... **RICHMOND**
19 January .... **WASHINGTON D.C.**
21 January .... **BOSTON**, Opera House

22 January .... **NEW HAVEN**, Woolsey Hall
23 January .... **BRIDGEPORT**, Poli's Theater
25 January .... **NEW YORK**, Metropolitan Opera House
26 January .... **ALBANY**
27 January .... **MONTREAL**, Théâtre St.-Denis
28 January .... **TORONTO**, Massey Hall
29 January .... **BUFFALO**, Elmwood Hall
1 February .... **ROCHESTER**
2 February .... **CLEVELAND**, Masonic Hall
3 February .... **SAME VENUE**
4 February .... **DETROIT**
6 February .... **INDIANAPOLIS**, Murat Theater
7 February .... **LOUISVILLE**
8 February .... **CINCINNATI**
9 February .... **COLUMBUS**, Memorial Hall
10 February .... **ST. LOUIS**, Coliseum
11 February .... **SPRINGFIELD** (Illinois)
13 February .... **CHICAGO**
15 February .... **GRAND RAPIDS**
16 February .... **MILWAUKEE**, Auditorium
17 February .... **MINNEAPOLIS**
18 February .... **DAVENPORT**

19 February .... **DES MOINES**
20 February .... **KANSAS CITY**
21 February............... **HUTCHINSON** (Kansas)
22 February............... **TULSA**, Convention Hall
23 February............... **WICHITA**
24 February............... **TOPEKA**, Auditorium
25 February............... **OMAHA**
27 February .... **CHICAGO**, Convention Hall
1 March .... **PITTSBURGH**, Syria Mosque
2 March .... **PHILADELPHIA**, Academy of Music
3 March .... **WASHINGTON D.C.**, National Theater
4 March .... **BOSTON**, Symphony Hall
5 March .... **SCRANTON**
6 March .... **NEW YORK**, Hippodrome
16 March .... **TRENTON**
17 March................. **HARTFORD**, State Armory
18 March................. **NEW YORK**, Carnegie Hall
20 March .... **PROVIDENCE**, Albee Theater
21 March .... **QUÉBEC CITY**
22 March .... **MONTREAL**, Théâtre St.-Denis
24 March .... **SAME VENUE**

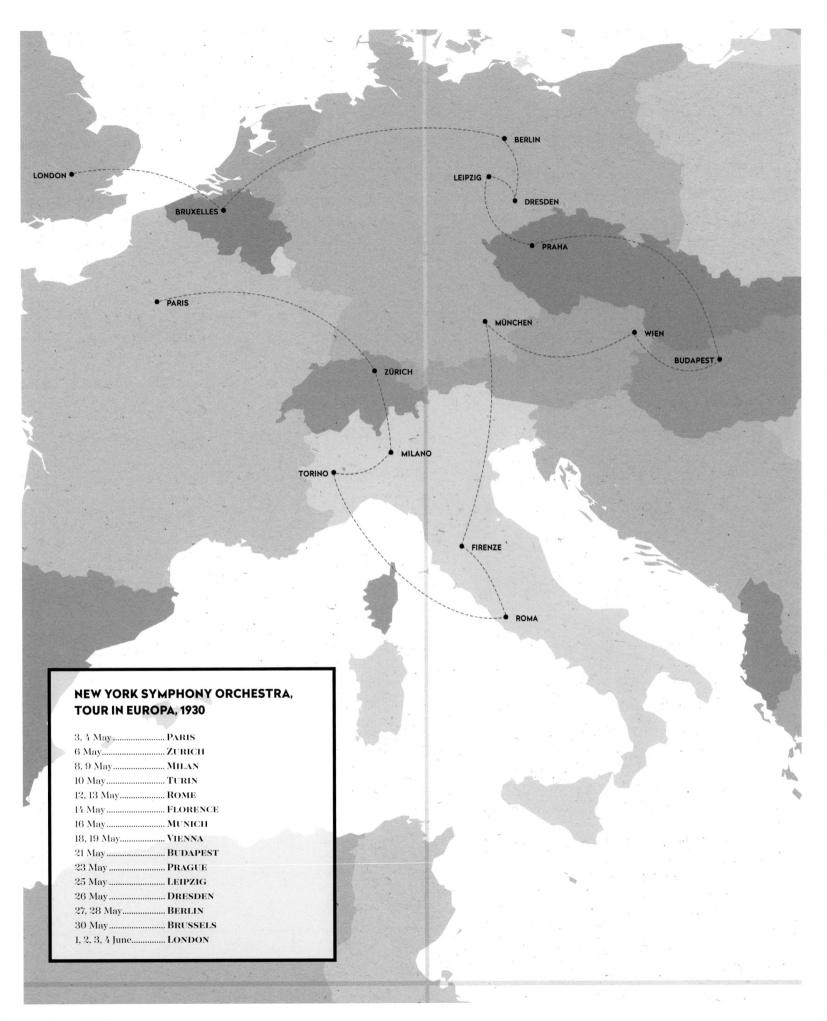

**NEW YORK SYMPHONY ORCHESTRA,
TOUR IN EUROPA, 1930**

3, 4 May .... PARIS
6 May .... ZURICH
8, 9 May .... MILAN
10 May .... TURIN
12, 13 May .... ROME
14 May .... FLORENCE
16 May .... MUNICH
18, 19 May .... VIENNA
21 May .... BUDAPEST
23 May .... PRAGUE
25 May .... LEIPZIG
26 May .... DRESDEN
27, 28 May .... BERLIN
30 May .... BRUSSELS
1, 2, 3, 4 June .... LONDON

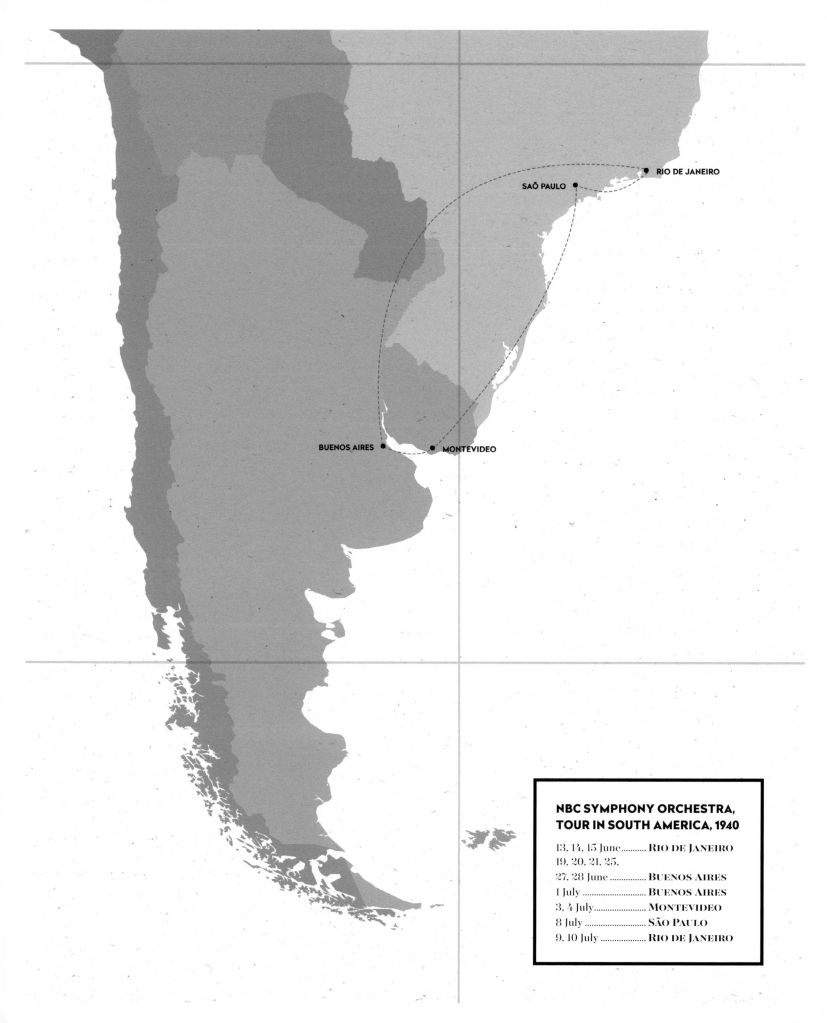

**NBC SYMPHONY ORCHESTRA,
TOUR IN SOUTH AMERICA, 1940**

13, 14, 15 June............ Rɪᴏ ᴅᴇ Jᴀɴᴇɪʀᴏ
19, 20, 21, 25,
27, 28 June .... Bᴜᴇɴᴏs Aɪʀᴇs
1 July .... Bᴜᴇɴᴏs Aɪʀᴇs
3, 4 July....................... Mᴏɴᴛᴇᴠɪᴅᴇᴏ
8 July .... Sãᴏ Pᴀᴜʟᴏ
9, 10 July .... Rɪᴏ ᴅᴇ Jᴀɴᴇɪʀᴏ

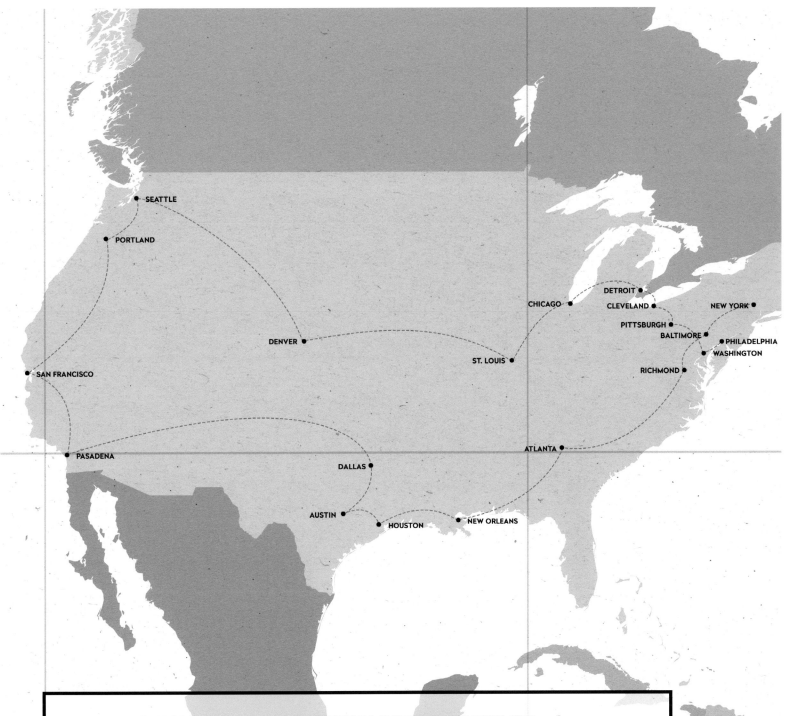

NBC SYMPHONY ORCHESTRA, TRANSCONTINENTAL UNITED STATES TOUR, 1950

14 April .... **NEW YORK**, Carnegie Hall
17 April .... **BALTIMORE**, Lyric Theater
19 April .... **RICHMOND**, The Mosque
22 April .... **ATLANTA**, Municipal Auditorium
25 April .... **NEW ORLEANS**,
Municipal Auditorium
27 April .... **HOUSTON**, City Auditorium
29 April .... **AUSTIN**, University of Texas,
Gregory Gymnasium
1 May .... **DALLAS**, State Fair Auditorium
3 May .... **PASADENA**, Civic Auditorium
5 May .... **PASADENA**, Civic Auditorium

7 May .... **SAN FRANCISCO**,
War Memorial Opera House
9 May .... **PORTLAND**, Public Auditorium
10 May .... **SEATTLE**, Civic Auditorium
13 May .... **DENVER**, Denver Arena Auditorium
15 May .... **ST. LOUIS**, Fox Theater
17 May .... **CHICAGO**, Civic Opera House
19 May .... **DETROIT**, Masonic Auditorium
21 May .... **CLEVELAND**, Public Auditorium
23 May .... **PITTSBURGH**, Syria Mosque
25 May .... **WASHINGTON D.C.**, Constitution Hall
27 May .... **PHILADELPHIA**, Academy of Music

PHOTOGRAPHY CREDITS

SOURCES

Alfredo Segre, *Toscanini. The First Forty Years*, The Musical Quarterly, n. 2, 1947.

Filippo Sacchi, *Toscanini*, Milano: Arnoldo Mondadori, 1951.

Andrea Corte, *Toscanini visto da un critico*, Torino: ILTE, 1958.

Samuel Antek e Robert Hupka, *This was Toscanini*, New York: Vanguard, 1963.

Luciana Frassati, *Il maestro Arturo Toscanini e il suo mondo*, Milano: Gruppo editoriale Fabbri, 1967.

La lezione di Toscanini. Atti del convegno di studi toscaniniani al XXX Maggio musicale fiorentino, edited by Fedele d'Amico and Rosanna Paumgartner, Firenze: Vallecchi, 1970.

Guglielmo Barblan, *Toscanini e la Scala*, Milano: Edizioni della Scala, 1972.

Harvey Sachs, *Toscanini*, London: Weidenfeld and Nicolson, 1978.

Gaspare Nello Vetro, *Il giovane Toscanini*, Parma: Grafiche Step editrice, 1983.

Joseph Horowitz, *Understanding Toscanini*, New York: Alfred A. Knopf, 1987.

Arturo Toscanini dal 1915 al 1946: l'arte all'ombra della politica, edited by Harvey Sachs, Torino, EDT/Musica, 1987.

Gustavo Marchesi, *Toscanini*, Torino: UTET, 1993.

Mortimer H. Frank, *Arturo Toscanini: The NBC Years*, Portland: Amadeus Press, 2002.

Harvey Sachs, *The Letters of Arturo Toscanini*, New York, Alfred A. Knopf, 2002.

Marco Capra, Gustavo Marchesi, Gaspare Nello Vetro, *Arturo Toscanini: vita, immagini, ritratti*, Parma: Grafiche Step editrice, 2007.

Vincenzo Raffaele Segreto, *Toscanini*, Parma: Gazzetta di Parma editore, 2007.

Arturo Toscanini: il direttore e l'artista mediatico, edited by Marco Capra and Ivano Cavallini, Lucca: LIM-Libreria Musicale Italiana, 2011.

TOSCANINI
The Maestro: A Life in Pictures

Rizzoli
NEW YORK

Texts and advisory
Marco Capra

Art direction
Stefano Rossetti

Book design and Layout
Rebecca Frascoli / PEPE *nymi*

Editor
Cecilia Curti

Editorial Coordination
Laura De Tomasi

Translation
Sylvia Adrian Notini

Iconographic Consultant
Carla Casu

Project Consulting
Maria Luisa Migliardi

Technical coordination
Sergio Daniotti
Sara Saettone

The publication of this book was promoted and supported by

We wish to thank Marilena Francese for her support and contribution to this work.

Cover picture: © Bettmann/GettyImages

First published in the United States of America in 2017
by Rizzoli International Publications, Inc.
300 Park Avenue South
New York, NY 10010
www.rizzoliusa.com

Originally published in Italian in 2016 by Rizzoli Libri S.p.A.
© 2016 Rizzoli Libri S.p.A./Rizzoli, Milan

2017 2018 2019 / 10 9 8 7 6 5 4 3 2 1

ISBN 978-0-8478-5922-1

Library of Congress Control Number: 2016956680

Printed in Italy